# BOWLING ENCHAN

# Bowling Enchanted Woods

## GORDON ALLAN

*THE*
*Alpha*
PRESS

Published by
The Alpha Press, 18 Chichester Place, Brighton BN2 1FF


First published in 1994



ISBN 1 898595 00 3

Typeset in Palatino by Grahame & Grahame Editorial, Brighton
Printed in Great Britain by Biddles Ltd, King's Lynn and Guildford

# Contents

No other game, Gauvinier was convinced, could so take on character (reflect it almost) from the person with whom you were playing, as this most ancient game of bowls. He sensed very dimly, but yet quite clearly, the reason why this should be so, though he could find no words to explain it: and knew that in sensing it, he was closing in upon the secret of the game's long hold upon people. The state of mind that gave a man's body the poise and sensitivity necessary for the delivery of a good wood was the state of mind which helped to free the imagination to bridge the gulf between one man and another.

Hugh de Sélincourt, *Gauvinier Takes to Bowls*
(Longman, Green and Co, 1949)

Signs near Worthing said "Pleasure Park" and "Leisure Centre" and "Fun Palace." In England, such signs spelled gloom. And yet Worthing, with its proud hotels and guest houses, did not look bad. It was a breezy, villagey place, with tree-lined streets, and like the folks who lived in it, Worthing was a little old, and a little lame, and a little stout, but it still had sparkle. It had the restful friendliness of a favourite uncle or aunt – lots of dignity but no airs, and a great deal of salty gentility and decent fatigue.

Paul Theroux, *The Kingdom by the Sea*
(Hamish Hamilton, 1983)

# Acknowledgements

My thanks to *The Times* newspaper and the magazine *World Bowls*, recently renamed *World of Bowls*, for permission to reproduce excerpts from material previously published; to the bowlers and bowling clubs who have unwittingly furnished me over the years with such a wealth of material; and to my wife for a number of valued suggestions.

The cover photo and the photographs on pp. 11, 31, 41 and 104 are courtesy of Stephen Line, Sports Photographer, Worthing. The cartoon, on p. 21, showing some of the Bowls Press, is by Simon Mundy. Cover design by Ian Wileman. I would like to thank Anita Grahame for her part in bringing about publication of this book.

# Acknowledgements

# CHAPTER 1

# *Trial Ends*

If this book shows a bias towards the ordinary club bowler, with the great champions appearing as the chorus rather than as the principal actors, then I cannot help it. I am an ordinary club bowler myself, fair to middling at best, inept at worst.

When I started in the game, I had ambitions, unconscious naturally, to be as good as David Bryant. Any bowler worth his Grippo has such ambitions at some period. But after the usual run of beginner's luck – club handicap and junior championship one season, losing finalist in the senior singles the next – I joined the massed ranks of those who never achieve anything of note on the green: a regular winner of matches, a born semi-finalist, a razor-keen competitor, somebody capable on his day of beating the club's best – and that's all. Why? Simple. Technique, temperament, luck – the great trinity that governs the playing of the game. One of those, two of those, all three, fail me at certain moments. They also fail Bryant and his kind, but less often.

Half of me, the sentimental half perhaps, belongs to Sussex, for my mother came from Hailsham; and now, every year, I spend several weeks of the summer in Worthing, a place once known to me only through some dialogue in Oscar Wilde. Every day, or so it seems, I reflect on the change made in my life by this game with the rather lugubrious name, bowls. Try saying it half a dozen times in rapid succession. In different parts of these islands it has a different sound, from "bowels" to "bools". It can be ponderous, comical, absurd, intense, according to accent and conviction. Guards officers and barrow boys might be speaking of different games.

1

In my youth in Aberdeen, during and after the Second World War, I knew nothing of the game. When I passed the bowling club in the next street I would glance through the green-painted railings at the men – the old men – at play, for it truly was an old man's game in those days; but that was all. The scene and the ritual did not register, except as things far removed.

When, a few years later, I worked for the local morning newspaper, it published a regular column on bowls, contributed by a man who had been a bank manager; his name was Donald Murray and he wrote under the pseudonym Jack High, which I subsequently discovered to be the commonest of all such names among the game's writers. It has the additional advantage of giving the writer's wife the cue to call herself Jill High, should she wish to break into print; my wife has used it once or twice, although I myself have never had to resort to pseudonymity. Donald Murray wrote well, in a style that would now be considered old-fashioned but was none the worse for that. Sub-editors bless correspondents who write well in any style, having to suffer so many who don't.

Editing Jack High's copy was my first insight into bowls, and somehow it brought me nearer to the players, the greens, the woods, the heads and the clubhouses than casual glances through railings at a few elderly gentlemen in caps and braces engaged in a stately pastime. But it was to be nearly twenty years before I set foot on a green.

It happened as the consequence of a whim. Living in north London, in Muswell Hill, and having for too long played no sport, I thought one day, for no particular reason, that I might make a decent bowler; my landlady knew the president of the nearest club – his name was Ernest Tyler, "Wat" to his friends; and I was in. The first singles I ever played was against "Wat", the oldest member of the club versus the youngest, for he was eighty-four and I was thirty-seven. What with my inexperience, his age, and the fact that we had been unable to enlist a marker, our match ran to three hours, instead of the average two, and I led for the only time on the end on which I claimed the match-winning shot.

I wrote down, on three separate occasions, my impressions of that baptismal season: "I have taken up the game of bowls. Yesterday I stepped on to a green for the first time, and for the first time rolled a wood up to the jack, or at least to its vicinity. I do not think I did badly: in fact I was told afterwards that I have a good style of delivery, setting the wood smoothly in motion and not bumping it, as many beginners apparently do. My chief fault, or rather the first of several to emerge, was an inclination to be too heavy: which is to say that I gave the wood too much velocity and succeeded only in depositing it in the ditch at the other end. Also, I did not give the wood enough green (how soon this sporting jargon adheres to your speech, like ivy): I aimed it straight at the jack rather than four feet or so to the left or right, to allow for the bias.

As for committing myself so far as to say that I enjoy the game, obviously I cannot. I shall find out in the next few weeks. My first day was cool, windy, and not too bright; I am assured that bowls is a different game when the sun shines. What I can say for certain is that today I am stiff and aching in various parts of my body. I am in such poor physical condition, by athletic as opposed to medical standards, that less than an hour and a half's timid exertion has left me acutely aware of muscles and joints that have slumbered for years. But never mind, little else could have been expected.

I have to ask myself, finally, why I took up the game at all. There is more than one answer. First, I need the exercise, and the small amount involved probably suits me. Second, it is a placid, contemplative type of game, and I am a contemplative person, though not consistently placid. And then, with my fondness for doing something a little different, it gratifies me to take up a game that could never, like squash rackets or football, be classified as fashionable, even though it is supposed to be played by more people than any other in Britain (which I doubt). The idea of bowls as an old man's (or woman's) game, to be played only when you are well past your prime and staring senility in its wrinkled face, can be disposed of by mentioning that Sir Francis Drake did not let a trifle like the Spanish Armada distract him from it; and he was no dodderer, whatever else he may or may not reputedly have been."

"I am not bowling as well now as I did when I started eight weeks ago. There must be a reason for this, and the only one I can think of, apart from the no doubt important fact that I am using old club woods which are a little too large and heavy for me, is that I have been given too much advice. Advice is helpful at the right time and in the right place, particularly when it comes from one expert. The trouble begins when you get advice from a number of experts. It usually conflicts, with the result that, since you do not know enough about the game to be selective, you become confused. This confusion communicates itself to your bowling. Instead of sticking to one style that seems to suit you, you conscientiously try to adopt the best features of several styles, and end, if you are not careful, with none at all.

One man tells you to fix your eye on a point on the other side of the green and aim for it. Someone else tells you not to fix your eye on anything in particular but just concentrate on a smooth delivery and an intelligent allowance for the bias. Up pipes a third oracle with the theory that you should hold the woods with your fingers, not cup them in the palm of your hand. But a fourth asserts that your grip is less important than it is made out to be and that a pendulum motion of the arm is The Thing. And, to confound you further, there is bound to be a voice raised to say that many players bowl well in spite of allegedly wrong techniques.

You cannot of course completely ignore what these folk say. All of them are right, up to a point. But there can be little doubt that though you, being a novice, must listen politely to their advice, you can safely let most of it go in one ear and out the other, trusting to the inscrutable law that enables you to retain instinctively only what you need. 'Playing it by ear' is more than just a phrase. From that point of view, the man who tells you about the bowlers who do many of the wrong things but still win, is the wisest of them all. In bowls, as in any other game, the secret seems to be to regard the commandments of technique as highly adaptable. If you do not, they will adapt you, until you are too rigid to improve."

"I now possess my own woods and need no longer feel like a superstitious cricketer forced to use someone else's bat. My woods took several weeks to come into stock, and as I was not entirely certain that I had made the right choice as to size and composition, the period of waiting seemed longer than it was. But I have found the new woods to be satisfactory: they fit my hand snugly and run well. I have won no matches with them yet, but they have given a better impression of my ability than the club 'cannonballs' I used to begin with.

I enjoy the exercise of bowling, which is not so gentle as it looks. Spend a whole afternoon or evening on the green, and you can be sure of getting rid of a fair amount of surplus physical energy. You bend and stretch; walk; bend and stretch again; and so it continues. The ritual is not convulsive or explosive. But the distribution of effort is even and healthy. In the pavilion the other week I heard a club member describing the miles he had covered and the poundage he had lifted in the course of playing forty-two ends. I cannot remember the exact figures, but they were not small, and they proved that bowls is not a game for the ancient. My attitude to games in general is that you either you play them because you like them, or you do not play them at all. To play them solely to keep fit seems stupid to me: you might as well run on the spot."

We beginners were called together in the evening by the club's captain, who, equipped with diagrams spread out on the clubhouse floor, and trenchant enthusiasm, instructed us in the fundamentals; and at the end of his discourse, gesturing to the honours board, he declared, "I didn't rest until my name was up there. Now I want to see yours there too." I think most of us achieved that much.

At length, and diffidently, I put my name down for my first match, against some club such as Bounds Green or Hornsey, Enfield Town Conservative or Potters Bar. They selected me as a lead. New bowlers are always selected in that position, though it is one of the most responsible in a four. Without a good lead a four is lost, more or less. My skip was Bill Rayment, a noted Middlesex bowler; I was nervous but had, I think, a reasonable game. If I make it sound too serious now, I can only say that that was how it felt at the time. It was my initiation into inter-club or social bowls, regarded by many as the heart of the game. I wore whites and a club tie, and dutifully tried to observe the niceties of etiquette, such as handing the jack or mat to my opponent, and keeping my distance from the head when the number three was in charge.

And afterwards I sat down to my first match supper – probably salad, which I abhor – and listened to the captains exchanging speeches and compliments, saying that the result did not matter, that the other team were as fine a bunch of lads as you could hope to meet, and so on, and on, until it only remained, in the old words, to be upstanding and drink a bumper toast to the "fine lads". Having seen the same supper and heard the same speech numberless times since, I have learned to be grateful for the jokes thrown in by the more knowing speakers as relief. For example: A player fell dead in the middle of the green, nonplussing the man on the mat, who called out to his skip for guidance. The skip, pointing to the body, replied, "Don't worry, just draw round him." Or: A bowler was passing a church when a funeral procession emerged, three men bearing the coffin. The bowler crossed the road and offered to take the fourth corner of the box, but they told him, "No, thank you, we can manage. You see, he was our skip and we carried him for years."

I came in time to look on these friendly matches as more a

duty than a pleasure. You have to be of a certain temperament – not mine – to enjoy them to the full. You must be sociable and fond of a drink or three. The bowling is secondary to what follows it – the first visit to the bar, the meal, the loyal toast, the oratory, the second visit to the bar, the evening of talk, punctuated by more visits to the bar. Some would sit there until morning if they had the chance.

Subject as I am to "cocktail deafness" – an inability to catch what the other fellow is saying in a crowded room – I time myself. I spend half an hour, at most, after the meal making conversation, asking my opponent stock questions about his club – number of members, condition of the green, and so forth. Then I make my excuses and leave, thankful for the evening air after the smoke and babble. If these occasions consisted simply of the bowling, with tea and biscuits afterwards, I would like them much better. Yet if that were so, they would scarcely be, as I said, the heart of the game for the majority of bowlers, when friendships are forged or renewed, business done, tradition honoured. Champions rise and fall, sponsors come and go, but the social side of bowls goes on for ever.

Friendly matches also raise the question of an old division in the game – between competitive and non-competitive bowlers. Competitive players, those to whom winning is paramount, tend to avoid social bowls, feeling perhaps that good shots played with nothing at stake are wasted shots: a curious notion if you think about it. This division can be seen, to varying degrees, in all clubs, and will always exist.

In *All About Bowls* (Hutchinson's Library of Sports and Pastimes) George Burrows, a good and prolific writer on the game, wrote many years ago:

"A man can only rise out of the rut of ordinary club bowls by proving that he has the match-winning spirit and temperament at singles. Because his club wishes him to take part in some trivial club game against a neighbouring side, and he should be competing in a county event, or a seaside tournament, is he to be stigmatised a 'pot-hunter'? Where is the real thrill in playing mere automatic bowls? A bowler who loves the man-to-man game and who is brave enough to go out into competitive bowls and get his share of defeat, ere he masters his own will and temperament, is to be praised rather than blamed. Skilful exponents of the singles game endure much from jealous club-mates. The four-a-side game certainly produces all that is good in friendly bowls, and promotes the team spirit, but it is not the beginning, or the end, of flat-green play."

# CHAPTER 2

# *Press Room*

Bowls is the only sport at which I have persevered as a player, but nearly ten years passed, from my first day on the green, before I began to write in earnest about it. It had occasionally occurred to me that I might combine playing and reporting, but I never acted on the idea, obvious though it was. Here was the opportunity to write on a subject I knew at first hand. Rugby I had covered, at that time, for twenty years, but my playing experience had been limited, and too often I was conscious of concealing my ignorance of some of the technical aspects of the game by cunning journalism – "writing round" the difficulties. The same was true of another sport I love, cricket, in which I dabbled for a while.

So, at the prompting of my wife, I took myself to Worthing one June weekend to watch my first tournament – the Masters singles – and send back eyewitness accounts. Bill Moseley was the winner that year, but he was shortly to become *persona non grata* because he was South African. Have no fear: I am not going to preach on that arid text, politics in sport. I will only observe that, given the strength of the game in South Africa, subsequent world championships and the like resembled Wimbledon without the Australians or Americans.

The press facilities at Beach House Park that summer were primitive. The little press room, next to the old pavilion, contained, if memory serves, a table, two chairs and a telephone, nothing else. They were like the stage props for a Pinter play. As I recall, we journalists had to dig around for the most basic information – players' names, ages, records – particularly during the August fortnight of the national championships, when there are hundreds of competitors.

All that changed with the cooperation of the English Bowling Association and the advent of enlightened sponsors. The press room now has three or four tables, sufficient chairs and telephones, liaison staff, a photocopier, player-profile forms, wall charts of results, a coffee machine, and other mod con.: reflecting in microcosm the greater interest the media has taken in the game in recent years. It is still difficult to coax sports editors into giving it the space its following deserves, but less difficult than it used to be, when the policy – if it merited so grand a name – was to send a features writer to Worthing or Leamington Spa once a year and regurgitate the stale, patronising stuff about Drake, an old man's game, David Bryant's pipe, exemplary sportsmanship, the women's figures. That is still done, but the patronising tone is muted now, and the real game – the players, the skill, the results – gets a reasonable showing during the main championships in papers that, obsessed with soccer, racing and boxing, once paid scant attention to what they regarded, complacently and erroneously, as a minority sport.

Bowls, played by countless thousands in many countries, is a minority sport, in any realistic sense of the term, only on the spectating side, since bowlers as a breed are not natural watchers; and unless you comprehend the subtler points of the game, and appreciate its slow-burn character, you can easily be lured into agreeing with the mockers who say it is as exciting as watching grass grow, paint dry or peas soak. However, for the sake of argument – and fun – let us allow, for the nonce, that it really is a minority sport. What must it do to turn itself into a majority sport?

Well, it must, as a matter of urgency, develop a suitable image. It must "put itself over". The image must be "macho". Out with white-clad figures in the parks. Out with sunshine and summer and cream teas. Out with sport and skill – and in with players hurling woods at each other and abusing

Summit meeting: the EBA Championships at Worthing.

officials, spectators burning deck-chairs and digging up the greens, and plenty of drug tests proving positive. Allegations of "fixed" matches and a few suspensions for life would also help, as would sex scandals and personality clashes. No sport worth the name is complete now without adultery and board-room disagreements. The adultery must always be written up as if it were unique, and the disagreements as if the directors had wrestled on the boardroom floor, when in fact hardly a voice was raised in anger.

With that image, bowls, or any "minority sport", would be followed as fanatically as football; and one day in the far future, the post-Bryant age, it would receive the ultimate tribute. People would start saying they were sick of the mindless hooligans on and off the green, that alcohol should be banned at big events, that they were frightened to take their families to matches, that the government should act, and that the game was finished.

But to return to the haven of that press room at Worthing. As I sit there on summer afternoons, gazing out on Vanity Fair, all sorts of unconnected thoughts go through my head. I wonder, for instance, whether the passers-by are curious about what is going on inside the room. Probably they are minding their own business. If they think about the press at all, it may be to envy us for having, in their view, such an agreeable way of earning a living – a view reinforced if they see us, with our feet up on the tables, sipping tea and munching cake – or to wonder how we managed to botch the facts in the morning papers.

Bowls is not, you see, a complicated game to report. It is advisable to watch every move in soccer or rugby, but you do not need to watch every wood in a bowls match. Come to that, you do not need to watch at all: it is perfectly possible to describe a match on the basis of the scorecard alone. The result will be colourless but statistically true, which, I regret to say, is enough to satisfy most readers. What can and often does happen is that you watch the last few ends and amplify with "quotes" from the players, which are unlikely, to say the least, to find their way into any anthology, but fill space and humanise the bits about back touchers and forehand tramlines.

I remember, in my greenery-yallery days as a sports reporter, covering a cricket match between Essex and Sussex at Brentwood. Ten minutes before close of play a celebrated Australian all-rounder of the previous generation, who was working for a national paper, made his first appearance in the press box, ascertained the facts, wrote his piece, telephoned it to the office, and returned forthwith to his hotel in Sloane Square. Something like that happens all the time in bowls. I have gone bathing in the sea during a Middleton Cup final. Others take to the golf course or browse in second-hand bookshops. But do not misunderstand us. We all love the game, though we may absent ourselves from its felicities awhile. And you love it too, you who read our deathless prose over breakfast next day.

Through bowls I have been introduced to press conferences and receptions, a world of which I had no previous experience, having led a sheltered, nocturnal life on sub-editors' desks and in printing-rooms. I have trodden the deep carpets of the Waldorf, the National Liberal Club, the National Theatre. I have been regaled with wine and smoked salmon sandwiches, requesting fruit juice instead of the first and devouring the second. I have been loaded with sponsors' information packs and free pens, and exchanged small talk with charming people. But I have declined to wear those identity badges, useful no doubt, that everyone else in my job hastens to pin to their lapels at sponsored events. I am not an exhibit.

I said that bowlers are not natural watchers of their own game, not in large numbers at any rate. I would also say they are not natural readers about it, either. Every village and club cricketer wants England to beat Australia, has firm opinions on the best team to do it, and opens his paper eagerly at the

Test match reports. The same applies, with even greater force, to soccer: any overweight, tabloid-reading Sunday-morning goalkeeper thinks he knows more than the England manager. But bowlers? You would be hard put to find one in a hundred who could name, say, all the skips in the latest England team, or the national singles champion. Most bowlers are parochial, with eyes only for their own clubs and competitions. If there is bowling on television, they will watch it – and soon forget what they saw. If there is bowls in their daily newspaper, they may not notice it, which is understandable in view of the fact that, apart from the main championships – and sometimes even with those – it is generally below the fold and so truncated as to be almost invisible. To that extent the regular bowls press corps, not a numerous body, has a disheartening time of it.

Nevertheless, as I have already hinted, there is a suspicion among the public that a bowls journalist's work – indeed that of any sports journalist – is not real work at all but paid recreation. This was brought home to me once on my own green in Surrey when my opponent asked me, between ends, what I do for a living. I told him and he said, without offence, "Oh, I don't count that as work – I mean, not like a carpenter or plumber." He did not say so but it was obvious that he saw true work as essentially manual, likely to leave dirt under the fingernails. Stringing words together on paper, although not his line, was yet easier than making furniture or laying drains. Any implement requiring as little physical effort to use as a pen must, on his reckoning, be inferior to a spanner or spade.

But also, I fancy, that man secretly coveted my sort of life. He would have liked to stroll into big sporting events with a nonchalant wave of an official pass, loll in the press seats, and avoid the crush. He would have liked the free travel, particularly if a day trip with the wife to Calais was a luxury to him. He would have liked – ultimate delusion – to meet the stars.

Now I am not going to pretend, for the sake of effect and to prove my bowler friend wrong, that a sports journalist's life is hard as a galley slave's or that its traps and difficulties are worse than the next honest toiler's. Far from it. Like most jobs, it is hard occasionally, routine the rest of the time, and interesting in a haphazard fashion. Nor would I pretend that meeting the stars is a galactic experience. Those I have met have been ordinary people with an out-of-the-ordinary sporting talent. Remove that talent and you are face-to-face with the man or woman next door, whom you probably cannot stand anyway. I do not see what else you could expect, unless you are gullible enough to think that every star ought somehow to be another C. B. Fry, who, besides having been a great all-round sportsman, could also have distinguished himself, had he been so minded, as politician, actor, barrister or author.

As for the travel, free or otherwise, I have to declare a prejudice rare among sports journalists. I enjoy pottering around Britain, but going abroad, under any circumstances, entails too many time-wasting procedures for my taste, whatever the supposed pleasures at the other end. Philip Larkin's attitude is the one for me: "I wouldn't mind seeing China," he told an interviewer, "if I could come back the same day."

# CHAPTER 3

# *People and Places*

It is the indoor game that, through television, increased public consciousness of bowls and its "quiet, connoisseurish element", to borrow a phrase of Peter Levi in the *Spectator*. I have often travelled to some event far from London, taken a taxi to the park or stadium, and in the course of conversation happened to mention to the driver my reason for going there; and he has told me that he has never played bowls but likes to watch it on the box, usually going on to ask me to remind him of the name of "that bloke with the pipe", and to admit he used to think it an old man's game but that more youngsters seemed to be coming into it now. These cab drivers, with their preconceptions, speak for the mass of the public. Without television, bowls would have remained hidden behind the hedges and closed doors of its clubs, in the popular estimation a pastime for greybeards, not the scientific, sinuous, highly competitive game it is now seen to be.

The earliest indoor championships I covered were held at Coatbridge and Hartlepool, and I might as well confess at the outset that I remember them less for the bowling than for the noise at my hotels. "What would you be happiest to have got away from?" Roy Plomley used to ask his desert island castaways. Many of them said the telephone. I myself would not say that, since the telephone is among the journalist's best friends. What I would say is unnecessary noise, by which I mean, in this instance, discos.

Now I have nothing against discos as such, but they must

be out of earshot, preferably in a different hemisphere, to earn my unqualified tolerance. At the hotels in question, which otherwise were habitable enough, the discos were so much within earshot that I could not read, write, think, listen to the radio, watch television, or – most important of all – sleep. I almost could not live, since the noise, magnified twenty times, in the wanton manner of all discos, made me feel suicidal.

At Coatbridge I returned to the hotel in the evening to find a disco starting directly beneath my bedroom. I endured it for a while, then rang the switchboard to complain, and they moved me for that night to a room in the other wing of the building. Even from there I was conscious of the dismal thumping, the harping on one note, the beat without the music. Once you have it in your ears, it is difficult to expel. It was at Coatbridge, too, the same week if not the same night, that I could not sleep for the television in the next room racketing away after midnight. When at length I managed to attract the attention of the occupant, and asked him to turn it down, he said he had not noticed it because he was asleep. I could only marvel at his powers of detachment, with or without liquid aid. I could not sleep with police chases going on at my bedside.

At the hotel in Seaton Carew, a mile or so along the shore from Hartlepool, the disco followed a wedding, and again it was immediately underneath my room. The disc jockey's voice was so loud that I could not hear a word he said. This time, when I complained, going down to reception in my pyjamas to do so, they transferred me to a different room until the disco ended early in the morning. There I did some work and, in between times, speculated as to whether the couple who had inflicted such suffering on innocent hotel guests deserved to live happily ever after.

How can a man take the fierce physical and intellectual

strain of reporting bowls championships if discos deprive him of his rest?

It is ever thus with me. The recollections from my work are not invariably those of winners and losers; I have seen so many of them, from Bryant to Joe Bloggs. That year at Coatbridge may well have been when young Nigel Smith beat Bryant in a world singles semi-final, a momentous match that converted quite a few people to the game and fired them to try it themselves. But although I remember the match for the context and the result, its details are lost to me, while I can still, in a sense, hear the purgatorial din of the discos.

Saundersfoot, on the Pembrokeshire coast, where I went for the British women's championships, stays in my memory for the moment of arrival. A colleague, Don MacQuarrie, and I, having by chance boarded the same train at Swansea, and with no knowledge of Saundersfoot, expected, in our naivety, a normal station in the middle of the town, with platforms, a buffet, and so on. We found it to comprise a single platform, a shelter, and a timetable. The only signs of life were cattle in the surrounding fields, birdsong, and a girl waiting for the up train from the west. Of the town there was no evidence.

We asked the girl for directions to Saundersfoot and she told us to go down the slope and turn left. We did this, expecting to see houses and people round the corner. All we saw was a road curving away through dense trees. There was nothing for it except to walk and hope, keeping to the side to avoid the traffic. After about ten minutes, by which time our suitcases were beginning to weigh us down, we came to two signs, one pointing left to Saundersfoot, the other pointing right to Saundersfoot. This was too much, and we thumbed a lift in an AA van.

We were lucky. Next morning two more journalists, Donald Newby and Gordon Dunwoodie, arrived, having had to trudge, laden with luggage, from the station into the town in warm weather, exertion for which they were not in training. We came on them sprawled on chairs in the pavilion, recovering over cups of strong coffee, and muttering about the pointlessness of having station and town so far apart.

Reverting to the moment of arrival. Nothing is more important to the peripatetic journalist than finding a good restaurant as soon as possible, wherever he happens to be. I know that, when I have found one, I go there every night. I therefore connect the Commonwealth Games in Edinburgh as much with a little Italian place at Tollcross as with Ian Dickison or Wendy Line at Balgreen. Indeed that restaurant comes back to me more vividly – unpretentious, animated, with Pavarotti or Domingo filling the air, and the chubby proprietor imitating them in snatches as he hurried among the tables. On my last evening I mentioned to him that I was returning to London next day; and he promptly announced the fact to the rest of the diners. He welcomed strangers as friends. The last time I was in Edinburgh I took my wife to Tollcross, but the restaurant had gone.

My favourite weeks of the year are spread over August and the early days of September, starting with the Bournemouth Open tournament, continuing through the EBA championships, and ending with the Worthing Open. It was the late Graham Howard, a former Guardsman and Surrey and England bowler, who encouraged me to go to Bournemouth and write about its famous tournament, the first of its kind, going back to 1909, and originally known as the Bowling Championship of the South Coast. In 1909 there were sixty-two competitors; now there are a thousand, and entries close twelve months in advance. Graham would claim that the Bournemouth singles was harder to win than the national singles; and he said that David Ward, the 1981 Bournemouth champion, gave as masterly an exhibition of singles play as he had ever seen.

Accordingly, my appetite whetted, I paid my first visit to Bournemouth in 1982, when Robert Provan won, and I have not missed a year since. The early rounds are played on sixteen or seventeen greens around the town but the finalists come together at Meyrick Park, a setting like a forest clearing; and the weather, in my time, has almost always been perfect on the concluding Saturday. For the finals I go upstairs in the pavilion and watch through the open windows of the locker-room, from where the trees, green, players, spectators, blue sky and sunshine make an effulgent portrait of the game at its best.

An even more spacious portrait can be admired from the balcony of the old pavilion at Beach House Park, looking across four greens, the ornamental flower-beds, the stands and the trees to the Brighton road and the sea. "It's incredible – we're paid to do this," Patrick Sullivan, the editor of the magazine *World Bowls*, casually remarked to me one fine lunch-time on that balcony, during the EBA championships: and in an instant I thought of one of my desert island books, *Autobiography* by Neville Cardus (Collins, 1947):

> "One day I sat on a table outside the little cafe at Lord's, talking to the cricket correspondent of *The Times*. The sun was warming all the world. The ground was animated. The pavilion was filling with notabilities anxious to get a good seat. As I sat on the table dangling my legs and enjoying a pipe and a cup of coffee, I casually said to *The Times* cricket correspondent: 'Has it occurred to you that we are paid to do this?'
>
> Paid to enjoy summer and cricket. I was also being paid to go after a day at Lord's to Covent Garden and hear Lehmann in *Rosenkavalier*.
>
> 'Yes,' said *The Times* cricket correspondent, 'it has occurred to me. And it's too good to be true, isn't it?'
>
> 'Yes,' I said, 'it can't last.'
>
> A few weeks after this remarkable and philosophical

*Back row (left to right):* Ronnie Harper, Don MacQuarrie, Gordon Dunwoodie, and the Author. *Middle:* David Rhys Jones, Donald Newby, and Patrick Sullivan. *Beneath the table:* Chris Mills.

conversation, Neville Chamberlain flew to Berchtesga-
den to see Hitler."

George Scadgell, a frequent winner at open or seaside
tournaments, called them the finest entertainment in the
game, combining the competitive spirit with the holiday
spirit; and he made a point of urging competitors to be sure
to go to the organisers, at the end of the week or fortnight,
and thank them for their work – excellent advice, as anyone
who has watched with admiration the multifarious activities
of the committee behind the scenes will appreciate.

A good secretary, it is said, means a good club. It is equally
true that a good secretary means a good tournament. He
has to be bowler, planner, diplomat, and humorist; and his
work is never done, for no sooner is a tournament over than
preparations for the next one begin. Without the dedicated
efforts, too often taken for granted, of people such as Dick
Jones at Bournemouth, Ron and Joan Prior at Worthing,
Dennis Cook at Eastbourne, and Harry Gold at Broadstairs,
these tournaments would not survive.

Every August I earn a handful of pens inscribed Worthing
Open Bowls Tournament. Thank You For Marking; and the
last bowl of the Worthing fortnight is nearly the last of the
summer for me, only the odd day remaining, at Oxford and
elsewhere, for the tidying-up, journalistically, of the season's
loose ends. With regret I journey home by train through the
Sussex country at sunset, past the croquet lawns of Southwick,
the boats of Shoreham, the roofs of Hove and Preston Park,
the estate agents' signs of Haywards Heath, the wings of
Gatwick. Soon afterwards, we all, alas, vanish indoors for
seven months.

Once, standing in full regalia, on the steps of the new pavilion
at Beach House Park, Fred Taylor, the president of the EBA
that year, offered to buy our dog, Figaro. Fred is from Cum-

bria, and Figaro would undoubtedly have been as happy on the fells of the north as he is on the commons of the south. Though grateful for the implied compliment of the offer, we declined it.

Figaro, a labrador-retriever cross, born in Norfolk, has been going with us to Worthing for the past ten years or so, and in his time has barked at David Bryant and been patted on the head by Tony Allcock. Another admirer of his is Jock Munro, the chief green-keeper at Beach House Park for many years, whom we first me in the spring of 1981, shortly before I began reporting on the game. Jock showed us round the pavilion, pointing to the names of celebrated players on the honours boards, and saying modestly, "I've beaten them all in my day. Bowls is a simple game."

Figaro has seen more bowls than most of his species but shown no inclination to retrieve the jack in his mouth, as has been known to happen with other dogs. During the British women's internationals at Sophia Gardens in Cardiff one year, three dogs rushed through the gate and cavorted about the green, threatening destruction to carefully built heads. That was also the year when a circus was in residence on the other side of the hedge in Sophia Gardens, and roars and grunts counterpointed the click of bowl upon bowl and the soprano cries of "Well played" and "That's the shot". It was a carnival of the animals.

Placid game though it is, bowls has its individualists, even its extroverts. Not all the players, or administrators, subdue their personalities in the interests of what might be thought a fitting decorum. Some give expression to character on the green; some off it; some wherever they are.

John Bell, a dark, brooding presence when he is playing, becomes a comic turn after the match. David Bryant, if he enters the press room, absorbs himself immediately in the play on the closed-circuit television, murmuring what shot he would choose in whatever situation happens to be on the screen just then: and thereby affords a clue to his pre-eminence, for great men in any field are obsessive. Wynne Richards, with his stammer, cannot help making people laugh. Mal Hughes, "the Durham Dancer", runs in a curve after his bowls as if biased himself. I saw and met the late Harry Reston only once – when he won the Bournemouth tournament pairs in 1984 – but his nose-to-the-green antics and cries of "Harry's trying" and "You're afae' well played, Harry" (he called his shouting release of tension) could not be forgotten by anyone who experienced them.

Then there is Bernard Telfer, the long-serving secretary of the English Indoor Bowling Association, with his fund of jokes and droll stories; and David Johnson, once a mathematics teacher, now the secretary of the EBA, and a Middleton Cup-winning skip with Warwickshire in his day, who was party to one of the more esoteric conversations to have occurred in the press room at Worthing. Arriving there one sunny morning during a Masters tournament, I answered the enquiry "How are you?" with "Twenty-four hours nearer eternity"; and for the next half hour I was able to sit back and say little more while my innocent remark was seized on and, with David leading, the talk soared away into regions where there are no bowling greens.

Of the press corps, Ray Potten has been reporting the EBA championships every year since they were transferred from Mortlake to Worthing. He and I compete to see who can perpetrate the first pun of the championships. There is ample material in the jobs and hobbies of the players. A coal merchant will make the right deliveries, a taxi driver find the best route to the jack, a quiz show contestant know all the answers, a watchmaker win in record time, using both hands.

The late Clarence Jones – Jimmy to his friends – was a Davis Cup tennis player who turned to bowls later in life, covering the game for the *Daily Telegraph*. He was the father-figure in the Beach House Park press room when I first knew it. Like the rest of us, he could not always attend every important event, and when that was the case he would obtain the results and details by telephone, so earning the nickname "Jimmy Phones".

Jimmy had been editor of *World Bowls*, which he founded, and his successor was Donald Newby, who also inherited the *Telegraph* post. With his white hair, craggy face and Suffolk accent, Donald is unmistakeable, a robust, industrious man, gruff but kind, who also devotes much energy to the running of antiques fairs. In the 1960s he stood, at two general elections, as a Liberal candidate for Eye.

Patrick Sullivan was head of the printing unit at the University of Kent before becoming the editor of *World Bowls* after Donald. If you like jazz, Pat, who plays the drums, is your man, a table-tapper in tempo, a whistler and a cigar-smoker: a man's man, in fact, who seems to have the priceless gift of getting on with anybody and everybody. He enjoys good Westerns, as I do, and when rain stops play – and even when it doesn't – we are as likely as not to talk of *Shane*, *Will Penny*, and *The Stalking Moon*.

David Rhys Jones, having been a drama teacher in a Bristol school before resigning to take his chance in full-time bowls journalism and television work, will talk as enthusiastically and knowledgeably of Samuel Beckett as he does of David Bryant. David was Bryant's pairs partner for more than a quarter of a century, and, like Bryant, is interested in everything about the game, from turf to tape measures. The Llanelli lilt in his voice can be detected, from time to time, in his writing.

Paddy Orr "lives" every bowl when he is playing and rarely discusses any subject except bowls when he is not. He was introduced to the game as a lad in Belfast, played indoors for England, and, in print, has an *alter ego* called Third Man. Chris Mills edits the magazine *Bowls International* and invests it with much of his own personality: brash often, dull never. Gordon Dunwoodie, based in Glasgow, but liable to bounce into view anywhere between Inverness and the Channel Islands, works extremely hard to keep the game before the public in the newspapers; as does Don MacQuarrie, also a Glaswegian, who now lives in Worthing. At Masters tournaments Don specialised in the overseas players' matches, and the press room lights burned late in the evening while he composed his copy on George Souza for Hong Kong or on Peter Belliss for Auckland. Like Donald Newby, Don used to be involved in politics, and he fought two by-elections in twelve months as a Scottish Nationalist.

Then there are those annual birds of passage, the columnists, award-winning or otherwise. They all, in their different styles, write the same things, sometimes quite nicely. One, I recall, descended on the EBA championships garbed in black like a Western gunfighter; soccer was his game and presumably he wished to awe the gentlefolk of Beach House Park with a hard-boiled image.

Having written his piece, in which he extolled bowls as a sport without unruliness, he returned to London. Unfortunately for him, later the same afternoon, after he had gone, a displaced bowl caused an altercation among the players during a fours match, David Johnson had to go out on the green as mediator, and the EBA took the unprecedented step of issuing official reprimands to both teams for their conduct. Nobody wants such incidents, but at least they may discourage the uninformed from writing as if all bowlers are paragons of virtuous restraint.

In national terms the *Daily Telegraph* has been "the bowler's newspaper" for as long as I or any player I know can remember. Walk into any club lounge in the land and as likely as not the first thing you will see is somebody reading it. Understanding the value of the game to its readership, it gives generous scope to the main events.

But for the most extensive, not to say exhaustive, coverage, you have to turn to the Pink 'Uns and Green Finals of the provincial press, a seam worked for many years by men like Ron Hails in the North and Harry Reynolds in the Midlands. There you will find, besides national and international championships, the chapter and verse of grass-roots bowls – reports, columns of results, league tables, the lot, with the "big names" mentioned in context and not blazoned as if no other bowlers existed.

# CHAPTER 4

# Matches

Anyone looking through the various writings about bowls would have to conclude it is not a sport that lends itself to lavish descriptions of notable matches, in the way cricket and football do. There have been numerous books and countless articles on coaching, on the history of the game, on its character and humour, on the careers of individual players, on clubs and countries, but none, as far as I have been able to discover, that chronicle, for instance, the best of the EBA singles finals since the championship was first played for in 1905, or at any rate since newspapers began to give serious attention to sport in general: for it is largely on contemporary journalistic accounts that we have to depend if we want to find out who won and lost this or that, as well as when and how.

Presumably nobody has considered such a book worth compiling. The quietness of the game could be a reason for this neglect: it does not hector, like football, or appeal to literary men, like cricket; and so it has been left alone to go its rather introverted ways, allowing many of its big men and occasions to be forgotten.

In that first EBA singles final in 1905, played at Upper Clapton, Jimmy Carruthers of Muswell Hill defeated James Telford of Newcastle West End 21–11, and their marker was none other than W. G. Grace, the first president of the EBA. There exists a photograph of the three of them: Carruthers jauntily wearing what appears to be a boater on the back of his head and looking like a mature schoolboy, Telford, with trim beard and formal hat, resembling a prosperous businessman, and Grace reminding you of nobody but Grace.

Both players were Scots, from Dumfriesshire. Carruthers was born at Lockerbie, Telford at Moffat; and I once met Dick Hayman, the last surviving member of the Muswell Hill club to have bowled with Carruthers.

"Jimmy," Hayman told me, "never smoked, never drank anything stronger than tomato juice, and never backed the horses, but he was partial to doing the football pools. He was a stocky figure, and a grand man on the green, good-natured, and full of the little tricks of the game – some of them would be called gamesmanship now – but of course fair."

Carruthers numbered his bowls one to four, as was then the custom, and the fourth had extra bias to give him a better chance of drawing round front woods when he was in trouble – something that would not be permitted now. He used the push delivery, having found that it suited him after breaking his right arm and losing a degree of flexibility.

My first sight of an EBA singles final was in 1974 when, on a random visit to Worthing, I saw Bill Irish beat Tom Wilkinson – the second time Irish had won the title, putting him in a select group who have won it more than once. But the first final I reported was Andy Thomson's 21–20 victory over Alan Windsor in 1981, one of the best ever seen. And for me there is a link, professionally a little embarrassing, between the matches of 1905 and 1981. Both were won by Scots (Thomson is from St Andrews) but my ignorance, at that time, of the game's history led me to write that "No records were readily available, but he (Thomson) may be the first Scot to win this event."

Remember that match? Thomson led 17–9. Windsor peeled at 17–17 and then crept ahead three times. On the decisive end, at 20–20, Windsor held the winner until Thomson moved it out with weight. Amid a hush Windsor tried to do the same to Thomson's shot wood and missed by what he reckoned to be an inch. Few had heard of Thomson until that day at Beach House Park; slim as a snooker cue, tall and pale, he was not long down from Scotland. Every bowler knows of him now.

During the Eighties two more players won the EBA singles for a second time – Chris Ward, adding to his 1977 success over David Goldring, and Wynne Richards. Ward's defeat of Bret Long in the 1982 final was not the most gripping of matches and I recall it only for a misprint. I described Ward as a printer who had been out of work for two years. This appeared as painter, and the headline announced "Chance for Ward to paint the town red" – something that might be difficult to do in Worthing. Richards – Welsh, bearded, and named after G. V. Wynne Jones, a rugby commentator on radio in the Fifties – beat John Kilyon in 1984 and David Taylor in 1986, the latter from a losing position of 11–18.

Twelve months on, the Beach House Park crowd settled down in the sunshine to watch what they imagined to be inevitable – Tony Allcock winning his first EBA singles championship. His opponent was David Holt, a bespectacled, sandy-haired, self-effacing lad from Bolton, with a crown green grounding in the fundamentals, who was even less known than Thomson had been six years before. Holt had already that week won the pairs with Tommy Armstrong but nobody gave him much chance against so experienced a hand as Allcock. Holt won 21–5 and Allcock described himself as "the unluckiest bowler alive" to have been confronted, on that of all days, by someone playing so accurately to the jack, bowl after bowl, end after end.

Allcock advanced to the semi-finals in 1989, losing to John Ottaway, the eventual champion, in a great match, and beat Kirk Smith in the 1990 final. He also won the triples with Andrew Wills, aged twenty, and Jack Drummond-Henderson, aged seventy-nine; an all-round man and sportsman, Drummond-Henderson – holder of a black belt for judo, a bowls coach for forty years, a fighter pilot in the Second World War, a worker for the Samaritans, to mention only a few of his sides. For Allcock these were his first EBA titles in eighteen years of struggle and pain, and they prompted him to say kind words about

Praying sometimes helps. Dave Kilner (Durham) appeals for guidance.

the Worthing greens, of which he had been highly critical in the past.

And now, what of the bowler's bowler, David Bryant? I saw him at Worthing win most of his nine Masters singles, but the records suggest that his prime occurred in the early Seventies, which was before my reporting time. He won the EBA singles in 1971, 1972, 1973 and 1975, and its indoor equivalent in 1971 and 1972. Consistency of that order has eluded him since then, partly because he is getting older and partly, it may be, because the opposition is getting tougher. He lost to Tony O'Connell of Wimbledon Durnsford in a semi-final of the 1976 championship and to Charlie Burch of Taunton in the final two years later – matches he himself has graphically, and revealingly, described in *Bryant on Bowls* (Pelham Books, 1985):

"I met Tony O'Connell in a semi-final which I shall never forget. Three times laying match when O'Connell delivered last bowls of the end, I watched him produce great saving shots on each occasion. Each time I could do nothing but praise him. Then I set up a fourth match lie, only to move the jack myself in an attempt to frustrate O'Connell producing yet another save . . . On the thirty-third end I wavered, so allowing him to deliver two potential scorers. With his fourth bowl he made it three, I failed to save the situation and for the first time in 185 minutes O'Connell took the lead 21–20.

Earlier he had won from 5–19 against G. C. Richards of Northants and in the final Bill Hobart reached 10–4 before O'Connell worked the crinkles out of his arthritic neck which had been aggravated by his earlier marathons and osteopathic treatment on the first day. Even with treatment, he was severely handicapped when striving for power. That he won the whole event was yet another chunk of evidence that if a player simply refuses to be beaten, then he cannot be beaten."

"Calm and unhurried, he (Burch) shrewdly varied the jack between thirty and thirty-eight yards from the mat and stuck resolutely to finesses. Using the draw shot as the foundation, he adorned this with gentle jack trailers, promotions and occasional in-offs that would have done credit to Steve Davis on a snooker table . . . On the day, his bowls were taking about nine inches more land than mine and I simply could not find the line for the jack at all . . .

After a long run I managed to get the jack and I promptly moved the mat up the rink. I got in with a two, promptly scored another two and then lay three shots; things were looking rosier. But there lies the reality of the game. One can be sitting pretty when, wham, the opponent produces a devastating shot that changes the position immediately. His destroyer was a dead draw on the forehand, his bowl winkling a way through mine to score a devastating single. I am used to dominating the play, win or lose. From that shot onwards Charlie controlled the play and I never looked like breaking it. He went on to win 21–11 and so was king for a day."

Strange to relate, I think I have seen Bryant only once in the EBA singles, and that was in 1982, when Clive Truscott of British Aerospace, Byfleet, beat him 21–19 in the second round. Truscott, with a textbook action, drew, drew and drew, and at the climax of a fine match, in front of a packed gallery, twice held the two shots he required to win. Twice Bryant killed the end. Then, at 20–19, Truscott pushed Bryant's shot bowl out of the reckoning, and that was it.

Bryant said that for his part he could hardly have bowled better. Truscott said he simply went out there to enjoy himself. Five minutes after beating Bryant, Truscott had to fall in again and play the holder, Andy Thomson, who won 21–5. Thomson went on to lose to Chris Ward in the semi-finals.

I enjoy browsing through the list of finalists in this championship and getting the resonances of achievement and disappointment. I like to see the names that will always toll like bells, such as Percy Baker and Bryant, the men who lost one year but returned to win, such as Algy Allen and Ernie Newton, or those who lost twice and never progressed so far again, such as Ted Redman and Tom Fleming – Fleming, luckless man, in consecutive seasons.

Baker was the bowler's bowler before Bryant, and their eras overlapped, with Bryant winning the first of his six EBA singles in 1960, beating Fleming, and Baker losing the last of his five finals, to Ralph Lewis, five years later. Baker, of course, was champion four times between 1932, when Bryant was scarcely out of his cradle, and 1955, and his 21–20 win over Algy Allen at Paddington in 1952 is sometimes used as a touchstone of bowling artistry; it inspired Jack Jones, the bowls writer, to this tribute:

> "It was a display that many old-timers who, like myself, had seen previous finals thought excelled all others, in fact the finest game they had ever seen. No end was without interest or sportsmanship. No shot, however good it appeared, seemed safe. Incidents were occurring in such rapid succession that one lost count of them as fresh ones followed. Shots we so often hope to pull off but so seldom do seemed child's play in these masters' hands."

I visited Baker's club, Poole Park, once, but he was then in his nineties, blind and unwell, and I was unable to meet him. They told me that, alone at practice, he used to stay on the green until he had bowled an end that satisfied him, all four woods tight round the jack; that he thought it madness to fire a lot; and that his memory for the game, like C. B. Fry's for cricket, was amazing, down to individual heads and shots in matches long ago.

Harry Shave, who won the EBA and British Isles pairs with Baker, wrote of him:

"I had the good fortune to be closely acquainted with him both on and off the green. His standard in all things was very high. He was also a very modest individual and a perfect gentleman at all times. I doubt if we shall ever see his like again."

# CHAPTER 5

# Grass Roots

---

## On with the Game

I was not present at the time but well informed sources assure me that nothing would have stopped Drake finishing his game on Plymouth Hoe. These days, the really difficult task is to get bowlers out on the green at all for an afternoon's roll-up. It is not that they do not want to play. It is rather that they do not want to desert the bar – that, and the dislike of your ordinary man for the mildest organisation and discipline: what he would probably call regimentation.

Say it is two-fifteen on a lovely July day. A few stragglers appear at the edge of the green. Let's get started. How many are we? Nobody knows, everybody guesses, in chorus. Is it odd or even? Could be even; on the other hand it could be odd. If it's odd, somebody might turn up at the last moment. If it's even, somebody might turn up and make it odd. Probably Alf: he always shuffles in late. Always was a member of the awkward squad. Cantankerous, that's what he is.

Alf's character having been dissected, attention reverts to the as yet undetermined number of bodies available for an afternoon's sport. There are five on the bank; at least as many again scattered elsewhere. A kind of roll-call *in absentia* ensues. Bill and Jack were last seen at the bar. Charlie was upstairs playing snooker. Brian's in the loo. Les said he was definitely coming but he hasn't arrived. George is phoning his wife about the dog. Mike's dashed home to fetch his woods, won't be a jiffy, forgot them, was in the county singles last night, see. Did he win? 'Course not.

How many ladies are there? Three. Groan. Click goes the gate. Ah, here's Janet. Good old Janet ("Not so much of the old, if you please"), now the ladies are even, they can have a pairs among themselves. That's one problem solved.

And still the men mill around like stray sheep. They need a shepherd, and here he is – Sam, the man who gets things done. Sam's bossy, Sam has a tidy mind. Every club needs a Sam. He's never the most popular chap because he gingers people up and organises them, which they resent even when it's good for them. Bit of a sergeant-major. Only wants a pace-stick (they mutter) to complete the likeness.

Sam rounds up the strays, gets them fell in in an approxima- tion to three ranks, does a quick head count, and announces a total of thirteen. Disaster. Thirteen faces fall. We're odd. Who'll drop out? Every man peeps at his neighbour. The gate clicks again. Enter Alf, taking his time as usual. Thirteen faces light up. We're even! For once Alf is a saviour and a hero.

Sam tells him to get changed pdq. Alf ambles towards the changing-room, mumbling that he's not going to be rushed, he's only a minute past the official starting-time. That's not the point, Alf, declares Sam. You're always a minute late. Why not leave home two minutes earlier and get here a minute before time, just for a change? Alf's out of earshot, though.

Playing-cards are produced to sort out a triples and two pairs. Ace to six the triples, and so on. I'm eight, who's seven? I'm a king, who's the queen? Babel. Someone has to draw a card for Alf, who's still inside wrestling with his shoelaces. At length the dust settles. On with the game, let joy be unconfined. The leads' coins glint in the sun. Is that your double-headed penny, Charlie? Alf heaves his first wood of the afternoon. It's tight and short, otherwise a good wood. Thin as a landlady's blanket, is one com- ment.

Up at the head Sam relaxes. Another good job well done. All

he has to do now is skip, child's play by comparison. Tiring game, bowls.

## A Superstition or Two

Superstition is not one of my weaknesses. I have read of an African crowd beating up a football team's goalkeeper because he buried a "juju" token in the back of his net, which they considered to be black magic. They went too far. People always do in sport, which is a breeding ground for superstition. Think of our own game.

"We've got them on thirteen now" is a daily cliché. Sometimes they stick on thirteen, sometimes they don't. It seems to me that they stick as often on twenty, if it's a singles match and the poor chap can't score the one he needs to win. For all that, nobody has built up superstition round the number twenty, although it could be argued that in bowls the case for doing so is more logical than the case for thirteen.

There are rugby teams who decline to number one of their centres thirteen and adjust by having the full back wear sixteen. I have come across a bowler who labels his locker 12a, like a first-floor flat. It prompted me to wonder what he does when his score reaches thirteen in a singles match. Does he refuse to recognise it? Does he give his opponent the shot, remain on twelve, and wait for the chance to leapfrog thirteen with a two? I mean to say, such a horror of thirteen could have regrettable consequences, like never getting off twelve and losing a final. I suppose this bowler averts his eyes from the scoreboard, grits his teeth, and carries on.

Now for the hallowed tea break. There is a sort of superstition about that, too. You've played ten ends in a club match and then you all troop into the pavilion's shade for tea and custard cream biscuits. Very welcome, too, I may say, adding that that's what I really put my name down for and the bowls is only an excuse to satisfy what Bernard Shaw called "the dipsomaniac craving for afternoon tea".

When you went in, your rink were leading comfortably. When you come out again, fed and watered, you find yourselves inexplicably on the slippery slope to defeat and can't stop. What's the matter? How could ten minutes off the green make such a difference? Your concentration's been interrupted, that's what it is, you decide, as if making an inspired discovery. The tea and biscuits are blameless. Never tasted better. It's the human element that upset everything.

The moral seems to be: if winning is important to you, don't stop for tea. Starve sooner than relax. Yet thousands would vehemently oppose the abolition of these tea breaks. I, for one, enjoy them too much. It's vexing to start bowling badly so soon after bowling well, but I prefer to think of my slaked thirst and those custard creams. Anyway, the idea that you always lose form after tea is superstition, and superstition is not my line. My bowling club is number thirteen in the road and the roof hasn't fallen in yet.

## Post-mortems

Coroners should make good bowlers. There are enough post-mortems in the game to keep them happy until their dying day. That is my conclusion after years of listening to, or overhearing, accounts of how Tom, Dick or Harriet won or lost, particularly lost.

> "I was two shots up and lying game, and had a blocker too, and one at the back, just for insurance you know, perfect position, and he fired, miles off target, a bad wood, and he wicked-in off a side wood, hit another of his own, and picked up the jack for shot, and that made it nineteen-all, and at the next end I was yards short, can't explain it, I was a mug, and he won with two jack-high

woods, should never happen, diabolical, another pint if you don't mind . . . ."

So much for the prosecution's case. Now harken to the defence:

"He was holding two for game, one in front and one behind, and I was up the creek, and all I could do was have a go, and it came off, 'cos I contacted one of my wing woods, played for it, see, and I trailed the kitty, that was nineteen-all, and I got two at the next end to win, bit lucky maybe, but I always say there's a lot of luck in this game and you make your own really . . . another shandy, please, George . . . "

As you can tell, the two cases are interchangeable. The only difference is one of emphasis. One man's bad wood was the other's winner. The shot "miles off target" was, according to the opposite interpretation, "played for". And so on. You believe who you want to believe, depending partly on your knowledge of the game and partly, perhaps, on which man you like the better.

I cannot be bothered much with post-mortems where my own performances are concerned – not aloud at least. I see them, so to say, as dead ends. Sometimes, when I lose, I think back over the match and remember what I did wrong, and where and how, and regret the chances I failed to take – the open draw when I was a yard and a half through, the yard-on shot I missed because I was too anxious to succeed. But I have never been one to spend the evening expounding it all in merciless detail to a semi-captive audience.

The same goes for matches I win. Naturally I am glad and, as before, I may recall in the night this end or that for its significance in the context of the whole. But speechify I cannot. It is more amusing to hear others do that – until I have had enough of it. If I do say anything on the subject it is generally

Obviously less than a short yard.

to the effect that my line and length were awry, if I lost, or, if I won, that my opponent had the same difficulties. I might also throw in the standard references to luck and the green. That, I feel, is as much as can be said afterwards about ninety-nine out of a hundred matches.

Let us therefore leave the locker-room, banish from our minds the epic match just ended, and make for the bar – where, if we are not careful, we may overhear somebody behind us, festooned in badges and waving a cigar, saying something along these lines:

> "I don't think I told you what happened to me in the championship last week, well, it was like this, we were even-Stephens, nip and tuck, until he got in front, at 17–15 it was if I remember rightly, and I was holding four – four, mind you – and he had the back bowls, and he came up with a firm one, a rusher the Scots call it, dead straight I'd say, those woods of his should be banned, and he got a bloody wick off . . . "

## A Short Yard

How long is a short yard? Nobody has ever been asked that on *Mastermind*. Probably only bowlers know the answer, and even then opinions could vary as to whether it is two feet nine inches, two feet seven and half, or whatever other vulgar fraction comes to mind in that pregnant moment when the man on the mat calls down the green to the marker: "How far is my last wood in front of the jack, Fred?"

Fred will probably need to be asked twice because he has one eye on the next rink where his wife is locked in combat with last season's ladies' champion. But when the voice of the man on the mat does reach him, he will advance to the head with a business-like hop, skip and jump, inspect it, announce as a matter of mathematical fact, "Short yard, Charlie", and remove any doubts (he thinks) by holding up his hands a short yard apart – more or less. Charlie will then adjust to the extent of laying his next wood a short yard behind the jack; and Fred will wonder why he took the trouble to give such precise information in the first place.

A short yard is indeed a much quoted distance in bowls. Not only is it less than a yard; it is also kinder to the player. A plain unqualified yard can sound like a mile to a man struggling to find his length. A short yard gives him a little hope, encourages him to think that next time, with luck, it will be shorter, perhaps be near enough to count.

Then there is a "a good yard". It is not so kind because it implies that the dreaded full yard has been reprehensibly exceeded. The "good" is not good, and must be bettered, or the skip will want to know why, with no excuses such as "Might be useful" or "Thought I'd try a blocker".

It is amusing to hear these various distances being sung out. I think of them as a sort of musical repertoire in which certain pieces are hackneyed and others rarely played. Any variation on a yard is as common as the 1812 Overture, eight inches an undiscovered masterpiece. Nine inches, on the other hand, you can hear any day, tenor, bass or soprano, and six inches likewise. As for one inch, it is a miniature, certain to do two things – cause a titter in the audience and make the performer tremble at the thought of trying to improve on a wood so adjacent.

Bowlers prefer round numbers that everyone, on green and bank, can grasp instantly. We can visualise a yard, two feet six, two feet, eighteen inches, one foot, nine inches, six inches, one inch. But to say two feet four and three-quarter inches or one foot three and an eighth, even in jest, would be wilfully to cause confusion and might be construed as liable to put the players off their game.

I await with interest the start of the revolution – the arrival of the metric system on the green. "How far is my last wood short of the jack, Fred?" "Short metre, Charlie." "Fred, I wish you'd speak English, mate."

## The Great Outdoors

If as a bowler I had to choose between perfect conditions indoors and perfect conditions outdoors, I would choose outdoor perfection every time. I think most bowlers would. A green running fast and true, with a good draw on both hands, and hot sunshine from a cloudless sky – that, to me, is a kind of paradise.

I say a cloudless sky, but it need not be so. A few wisps of cirrus are restful decoration and present no threat. Since taking up the game I have developed a close interest in cloud formations and become quite a judge of them. Before that, it did not matter much to me in summer if the weather was fine or wet. I preferred it fine, naturally, but if it was wet I was stoical. Now, if it is wet, the stoicism is put to a severe test.

At daybreak I part the curtains and see with relief that the sky is clear and bright. For once, I remark, the forecast is accurate. I can play this afternoon as planned. But during the morning nimbus clouds gather. The blue disappears. All is grey and heavy; the clouds are as much cumulus as nimbus – have I the right terms?

Cumulus, nimbus, or whatever, the clouds start spilling rain, which thickens and persists, going on long past lunchtime. Pools of water form an archipelago on the green. We – the eternal optimists who have turned up – sit looking through the long windows of the clubhouse, waiting for the rain to stop, exchanging small talk, and vilifying the meteorological experts for being wrong again: they said nothing about rain later. The rain does not stop until after we have gone home, and then the evening turns out lovely.

Everybody who was there remembers the hailstorm near the end of the 1983 Masters final at Worthing, when David Bryant and George Souza came off, went on again, and Souza won, the woods making spray as though they were the prows of ships. My first year at Worthing was 1981; the sun blazed down for the whole fortnight of the EBA championships and the sea was warm at midnight. I was dazzled into imagining every championships fortnight was like that, but since then I have often sheltered in the Bowl Inn, questioning the very existence of summer. "More than just sunshine", say the Worthing advertisements; and that's the truth.

Bryant and Souza played on, but theirs was a special case. We come off and stay off when heavy rain, let alone hail, begins. We have all, of course, played competition matches to a finish when it was wet. It gives us an excuse for losing, if nothing else, and if we win it allows us to say that all conditions come alike to us. But nobody enjoys it. If we wear glasses we have to keep wiping them, which is a nuisance, and the woods are difficult to grip.

I know players who would concede a competition match rather than start in bad weather. Though I am not sure I agree with them, I see their point. Yet I certainly do not agree with those who say bowls should never be played in the rain because it makes a lottery of skill – rather echoing Bradman, who, asked about his dislike of bad wickets, replied that Inman did not expect to play billiards on a torn table. Bradman's analogy was inexact. Rain and bad wickets are facts of life. Bowlers averse to rain to that extent should confine themselves to the indoor game. Give me the outdoor – rain or shine.

## Pot-hunting

Some of us know of couples splitting up, or threatening to,

because the pot-hunting husband spends longer on the green than he does at home. Part of the trouble, in an exceptionally time-consuming sport, is that there are too many competitions, too many temptations to put your name down just once more to oblige a friend by making up a pair, triple, or rink.

Think of those proliferating competitions. What other game accommodates so many variations on one simple theme? Besides orthodox singles, pairs, triples and fours, you have two-wood singles and triples, mixed pairs, mixed triples and mixed fours, championships, cups, leagues and tournaments without number, all the way up from the clubs, through councils, towns, cities, regions, county areas and counties, to national, international and world level, with new events being born regularly and sponsors hoping to suckle the infants. For all I know, there may be a one-wood singles somewhere.

Here is a scene easy to imagine. The young bowler, husband and father (in that order) dashes in from work. Steak and kidney pie, his favourite, is on the table, but he does not seem to notice, and runs upstairs, coming down almost at once, three steps at a time, clutching his bowls bag.

"Sorry, can't stop tonight, luv," he says, a little out of breath. "Got a match, see."

"Now what is it?" she asks wearily. "Don't you realise you've been out every day this month?"

"Mills & Boon unisex mixed fours prelims," he replies, opening the front door and groping for his car keys.

"Never heard of it. You didn't tell me anything. Have you really got to play?"

"It's a great new competition – lots of county players. Bye."

No kiss. The door bangs. The car roars away. Later in the evening, the baby asleep, the wife casually switches on the television and finds bowls there. She switches off at once. It is too much.

## Bless the Marker

There are times when I am convinced that finding a marker for a singles is much more difficult than playing the match itself. It can certainly take longer. It is not the fault of the first dozen people you ring up if they are otherwise engaged on the day in question, and you try to sound relaxed and understanding as one by one they excuse themselves; but a feeling of persecution can creep over you.

The great occasion is the first round of the club handicap, which you have been striving to win for ages. You think: this could be my year, I'm in the easier half of the draw, the old arm is working well, and my immediate opponent is a novice bowler. The match is in the book, the rink reserved. All that remains is to arrange a marker. Shouldn't be difficult. Big membership. I'm on good terms with most of them. Couple of calls at most should do it, if I don't happen to meet a willing soul in the locker room first. Such is confidence – a deceitful jade.

Steve, who often marks for you, as you do for him, says he'll be on holiday, and you can't expect a man to rush home from Florida just to mark a game of bowls. Mike's got a match himself that evening. It's Tony's wife's birthday and if he wants to stay married he'll have to wine and dine her. Brian suddenly remembers he's on night shift. Phil has to visit a rich aunt in hospital. Tom's into amateur dramatics and he'll be playing Sherlock Holmes (you want to ask which competition). Dave has a broken wrist. Fred has to see a man about a dog – really. Jim's not bowling this season – domestic pressure he calls it, volumes of dark meaning in his voice. Peter's moving house (what – again?). Eddie can't make it because his car's up the spout. George couldn't be back in time from a funeral.

At which point you think you have come to a dead end, until you remember the ladies, but decide you had better not because for some obscure reason some players don't like being marked by the opposite sex, although they ought to be grateful to have a marker at all, and leave sex out of it.

You then count the number of potential markers you have approached, sigh, pick up the phone for – what is it? – the thirteenth time, persuade Arthur, the club's oldest member, that he has no pressing business on the evening of your match – no assignations in the West End, no heart transplant surgery to undergo, nothing – and he utters the magic words: "Yes, I'll mark for you, old son, it'll be a pleasure." At that moment you want nothing so much as to remember Arthur in your will.

## The Tea Question

Of all the pleasures of an afternoon on the green, not the least is the cup of tea afterwards. It is nearly always made by the ladies, and loud are the votes of thanks to them for their trouble. In fact, without the ladies there would probably be no tea at all because some men, although capable of building a house with their bare hands or taking a car to pieces and putting it together again, shrink in terror from boiling a kettle of water and popping a few teabags into the pot. Could it be that they honestly do not know how to do it? That they leave everything to their ever-loving wives at home? That they consider the job too menial for them?

These are deep matters, involving psychology, social distinctions, guilt complexes, and goodness know what else. I have no wish to paint the great race of bowlers either as whiter and finer than their fellow-men, or as blacker and more devious, because obviously that is not the case. But I cannot help wondering if those votes of thanks to the ladies for making those life-saving cups of tea at the end of a scorching afternoon's bowling are not also oblique expressions of relief by the men that they themselves have been spared the work.

I have noticed, too, that when there happen to be no ladies around, the men are quick to assure one another that the supply of teabags has run out, or that the gas has been cut off, or that the milk and sugar must on no account be touched because they are needed for match refreshments in the evening. It may even be alleged that the kitchen is out of bounds to the men and that the ladies would be angry – might take industrial action to the extent of refusing to make the tea any more – if they knew their spouses had trespassed in the holy of holies.

But this tea question is not just parochial and funny ha-ha. There is another side to it. In some clubs the ladies are not allowed to play bowls but are allowed, indeed encouraged, to do the indispensable domestic work behind the scenes, including making the tea and cooking the meals. I have heard men at one club say with some vehemence that if the unthinkable happened and women were allowed to play on their green, they would resign on the spot. And I have no doubt they speak for the men at all the clubs where women can wash up but not roll up.

There is no good reason that I can think of, least of all tradition, why women should be barred from playing in this way. If the men can share a bed with them, they can surely share the green. If I were a woman and wanted to bowl, I would not let myself be used exclusively as a cook and bottle-washer by the monstrous regiment of men, no matter how fulsome their gratitude ("The Ladies – God Bless 'Em!"). I would be prepared to help with the work but only on condition that I was allowed to bowl. That is common sense and fair play.

What is needed is a sort of women's liberation movement at those prehistoric clubs where they are still not allowed on the green. A start could be made with an ultimatum to the men: No bowls for us, no sausage and mash for you.

What committee, however fossilised behind all those Wolf Cub badges, could resist that?


## Season's End

The end of the outdoor season is a sad time and one of the saddest things about it is the premature way the green empties. It is curious as well as sad. The spate of competitions has long dried up, finals day has come and gone, and yet these should not be reasons for all but a handful of members turning their backs on the old place until next May.

Our summer is short enough, you would think, to prompt every bowler to squeeze every drop of enjoyment he can from it, without troubling himself about whether he is playing for some bauble or other. But no: off they go, most of them, early in September, taking their woods with them, perhaps, in preparation for the Great Indoors, returning only for the Christmas party or a game of snooker.

I say good luck to them ironically. To those few who stay on and play to the last moments of the season – the last weekend in September, the first in October – I say it gratefully. In my book they are the true enthusiasts. They were there – remember? – at the end of April, when the green was heavy as a mown wet field, and woods heaved with all their might stopped yards short. They were there in midsummer, when it was difficult to find a vacant rink, especially in the evening, because of the sound and fury of competing competitions. And they are still there, as aforesaid, at the end of September, rolling up as usual and just as keen. They probably didn't win as much as an egg cup in the competitions, but they don't let that overshadow their pleasure.

Recalling their first roll-up of the season in April, they always say: "Crikey, hasn't the summer gone quickly. It seems only yesterday . . . " And of course they are right. The summer does go quickly, too quickly, even when it is a wet one, which is often. But if they add that they're looking forward to bowling indoors, you know, if you have an ear for nuance, that they only half mean it. The indoors is all right, good for keeping your hand in, and beyond question skilful, but it must always be a substitute, second best. It lasts seven months and, unlike the outdoor, never goes quickly, a fact only partly explained by its length and its conjunction with winter.

There is an altogether different note, a heart-felt note, in these same bowlers' voices when they tell you, at the end of the indoor season, that they're looking forward to getting outdoors again. They mean it, my goodness, they mean it.

# CHAPTER 6

# *Pot-pourri*

Players like me go on, season in, season out, hoping for but not expecting better things; entering for competitions we have scant chance of winning; now and again making a perfect draw to the jack or hitting dead-on with a drive; sunning ourselves on the south coast; learning that old Stan has passed away or that young Phil has got his badge; changing woods but finding our standard remains the same; marvelling at the man who has been using the same set successfully for forty years; threatening, in moments of despair, to give up the game but always returning for more; trying to convert others to it while realising how silly it must look to the uninitiated, who much prefer shopping.

Yes, we know, all games are silly. But it has to be conceded that bowls can look sillier than most, with its affinity to marbles and its lack of physical expression. It has its mystique, though, like any game: some element that even the players cannot explain but which they unashamedly invoke, knowing they cannot be contradicted.

And it is, as much as football, the people's game. To prove it, open the EBA *Yearbook* at the section listing all the affiliated clubs under their counties. Almost any page will do. I open the book at random and drop into the middle of Essex, which suits the purpose admirably, for there I find the STC/STL (Harlow) club, whose address is STL Laboratories, and, a little lower down, Tate & Lyle, United Services, Walthamstow Trades Hall, Warley Hospital and Wickford Royal British Legion. Durham opens at Darlington Railway Athletic, Dean and Chapter Welfare,

Durham County Constabulary and Hartlepool Catholics, and Norfolk at Downham Market Conservative, Norfolk County Council, Norwich Union and Wissington Factory. Leicestershire has Burgess Parish Council, Hinckley Sweet Pea, Leicester Telephones and Rolls-Royce, while Gloucestershire has Bristol Aeroplane, Cotswold Strollers, ICI (Fibres) and National Smelting Company.

Truly a classless game, a people's game. Office workers, manual workers, scientists, railwaymen, nurses, policemen, freemasons, bus drivers, telephonists, civil servants, gardeners, journalists, people with political and/or religious convictions, people with none – they are all there, in fact or by implication. In an EBA singles final not long ago the winner was a coal merchant and the runner-up an electronics research officer.

Some clubs have put down their roots in unlikely places, as much as to say "This game belongs to everybody, everywhere – duke and dustman, poet and peasant, town and country." One of my earliest discoveries was the City of London club in Finsbury Circus Gardens, behind the commercial palaces of Moorgate. Along the street in Finsbury Square you can see office workers and pensioners rolling up on the public green in the lunch hour, but that is just outside the Square Mile. The City of London is a proper club, established in 1924 and now open to all; until 1978 you had to work in the City to be eligible for membership.

There are unusual features about the club, apart from its location. The land it occupies formed part of London's first public park in the seventeenth century. The green was used as a barrage balloon base during the Second World War. On the site of one of the buildings overlooking it stood Bedlam before its move to Lambeth. There is a bandstand on one side of the green, two metal chess boards (bring your own pieces) on the opposite bank, an old drinking fountain in a corner, and a public wine bar and restaurant next to the pavilion.

Not far away, in an even stranger setting, can be found the Tower of London club, in the moat opposite HMS Belfast, where some of the Yeoman Warders play visiting teams such as the Chelsea Pensioners and the Honourable Artillery Company on Wednesday evenings during the summer. It must be the best guarded green in the world, thanks to the Warders, the Army and the ravens. It must also be one of the most curiously shaped, being oblong and uneven, allowing corner to corner play by two rinks of five players each, or up and down by three rinks of four each.

No cut-throat competition at the Tower, no heads rolling, no post-mortems in the Yeoman Warders' Club. They bowl for the fun of it, nothing else. All the Warders are ex-Servicemen and they want a game, not a war. There is no measuring for shots; dress is optional; the player who finishes nearest the jack on one end always delivers the first wood of the next; and having once been "shushed" into silence at a club where a singles match was in solemn progress on a neighbouring rink, the Warders decided that in future they preferred home fixtures.

From Edward I, said to have been the first English king to play the game, around the turn of the thirteenth century, to the Princess of Wales opening an indoor club at Luton a year or two back, bowls has numerous royal connections. The Royal Household club in Home Park, Windsor, down the hill from the Castle, has been carrying on the noble line since George V bowled the first wood at the opening of the green in 1922.

Only past or present staff of the Royal Household, employees of the Department of the Environment, the police and their families can join, along with a few associate members; and they have the extra responsibility of representing a club that touring associations and clubs from all over the world want to visit and play. About fifty applications for fixtures are received annually, which poses a delicate problem for the secretary.

So it is a club like, and yet unlike, any other. In its singles championships the men play for the King George VI Cup and the ladies for the Duchess of Kent Cup.

"Today," wrote an anonymous contributor to Godfrey Bolsover's monumental encyclopaedia of the game, published in 1959, "bowls of one sort or another has adherents in all of the English-speaking countries, and the game is played by more people than any other." (The people's game, you see.) And he goes on, with a charming touch of irrelevance: "It is a game requiring skill and dexterity, and the following quotation from 'The Best of England' by H. A. Vachell suggests that it could require considerable energy too:

> "On the fourth of August, 1739, a farmer of Croydon undertook for a considerable wager to bowl a bowl from that town to London Bridge, about eleven miles, in five hundred times, and performed it in four hundred and forty-five times."
>
> "Mr Vachell comments: 'This works out at forty-four yards a time, no mean achievement when we consider the condition of the roads of that day and the inevitable bias of the bowl. There was, however, no congestion of traffic then.'" (Quotation from Godfrey R. Bolsover, *Who's Who and Encyclopedia of Bowls*, Rowland Publishers Ltd, 1959)

Now to sportsmanship. Much nonsense is spoken and written about the supposedly exalted standard in bowls, making the game sound insipid, as if played by bloodless curates. I have seen good players who hated losing leaving the green in a hurry after a defeat, without shaking hands with their opponents or offering to buy them a drink, and disappearing into the night. You cannot condone such behaviour, but at least it shows the human side, and rescues the sport from preciosity. A minimum of ostentation is one way – a quiet "Good wood" or "Well bowled", or a couple of handclaps. The other man's bowls are challenges to be met, not objects of indiscriminate, perhaps insincere, admiration. I have read somewhere that Peter Line may praise his opponent after a match but rarely during it, and that is another way, a hard but fair thing to do. As Line said, why offer gratuitous encouragement to somebody you are striving to beat?

Lastly, some suggestions for changes in the game, bearing in mind the perennial complaints of a gulf in communication between players and administrators, that the players' views are ignored. Twice I made a selection of these views, from biographical forms at the EBA championships, and noted recurring requests for players to be allowed to change positions during team matches, for the laws to be rewritten in plain English – and for the game to be left as it is. Here, verbatim, are others:

- *Restrict players continually running after their bowls to the head.*
- *Do away with rink strings – they generally hinder more than help.*
- *Abandon wearing of ties in county matches. Anything more archaic I cannot think of!*
- *Stop chalking woods. Many bad woods hit the jack, many better woods end closer but do not receive any such advantage. Remove all woods from the ditch other than a wood that actually carries the jack into the ditch – hence no chalk required.*
- *Make the Middleton Cup a knockout, drawn round by round.*
- *Bigger jacks.*
- *Bowls only to count within six-foot radius of jack.*
- *Allow shorts to be worn in outdoor game.*

- *Every club to have a map of their own county, depicting all clubs within that county, to enable new members to locate away fixtures.*
- *Less basing of finals and invitation tournaments in the south.*
- *Flood-lit bowls.*
- *Have one standard bias so that every bowler has the same chance.*
- *A complete and utter distinction between professionals and amateurs. Professionalism has done nothing for the game.*
- *Introduction and ratification of all-weather greens.*
- *Option of four trial ends in county/national competitions.*
- *After winning an end, you should have the option of giving the jack away, leaving you with the last wood.*
- *No time limit on games.*
- *Penalise firing jack off green . . . it's like upsetting the pieces on a chess board when things get impossible.*
- *Three drives only per game – to be starred on card.*
- *Grade outdoor greens, thus improving the general standard.*
- *More of entry fees and sponsorship should be returned to the players.*
- *Cut out excessive congratulations after delivery of woods.*
- *Triples to be a two-wood competition and twenty-one ends.*
- *More relaxed dress code for women.*
- *The introduction of coaching to schools, to start bowlers at a younger age.*
- *Try and rid the game of people who shout "Hit it hard", "Get through the hole". Also try and remove*

*time-wasters.*

- *Outdoor clubs to go more up-market. Encourage clubs to improve off-green facilities, similar to golf, even if it means increasing subscriptions.*
- *Higher banks so that the jack doesn't go off the green.*
- *Implement penalties for abusing the rule relating to possession of rink.*
- *More aggressive marketing and administration, better press coverage.*
- *Education of all bowlers as to the laws of the game.*

# CHAPTER 7

# Portrait of a Bowler

Let me introduce you to Uncle Fred, waving his pipe and his pint. He is a squat man with red cheeks and a neat moustache of the kind often described as military. Everybody, inside or outside his bowling club, calls him Uncle Fred: many, indeed, either don't know his surname or forgot it years ago; some just call him Uncle.

The word uncle suggests benevolence but there is not a great deal of obvious benevolence about Uncle Fred. He is too waspish for that, especially in matters relating to his club, of which he will, one day soon, be the oldest member. Every club needs an oldest member (perhaps that should be Oldest Member), in the same way that every club needs a badge, and Uncle Fred will be a credit to the position when he attains it. He will certainly be the proudest and worthiest member, never having belonged to any other club, and having in his time been president, chairman, secretary, treasurer, captain, match secretary, competition secretary, press officer, green ranger and champion, not to mention bar steward when one incumbent left without notice.

There is a long tradition of bowls in Uncle Fred's family. "It runs in the blood like a wooden leg", he has remarked countless times, with a chuckle, quoting a quaint saying of his father's. His father and both his grandfathers belonged to the club, and his mother was ladies' champion not long before she died. His brother, also a good bowler, was killed in the war. Uncle Fred joined in the year he became eligible for the vote. He had been advised to start young – young in bowling terms, that is – and he did. He has had the same locker number – 77 – ever since, and become very attached to it, so much so that when, during extension work, he was asked if he would mind changing to 79, he was indignant.

That's Uncle Fred for you. A man of firm opinions, even on locker numbers. It's the same with him on the green. Once he's decided which hand to play, nothing and nobody, least of all a skip, will induce him to change it. Inflexible, maybe: but he's got his name on the honours board more than once, and that proves something. Uncle Fred has proved a lot of things in his lifetime with the club, as you will find if you read on.

*     *     *

Uncle Fred lives a few doors from the club, which enables him to keep an eye on things. A few members think his presence too pervasive; they say that even when he's far away on holiday he still *seems* to be at home, in or around the clubhouse. "It's spooky", they've been known to mutter, half resentfully, half (though they'd never admit it) admiringly.

His house resembles a bowls museum. Every room contains something connected with the game, even the bathroom, where the picture on the drinking mug shows bowlers at Beach House Park. In the living-room there is a large water-colour, signed Douglas E. West, that Uncle Fred bought in The Lanes in Brighton. It depicts a roll-up at a village club, probably in Sussex, possibly somewhere such as Steyning, of which Uncle Fred is particularly fond. Although the atmosphere is well caught, some of the detail, to Uncle Fred's fastidious eye, is wrong: the green mown straight up and down instead of diagonally, no mat, and the players' headgear making them look more like golfers. But the lignums, the pipes and the postures are authentic, and Uncle Fred appreciates the picture's merit as an affectionate piece of impressionism. He calls it restful and enjoys looking at it on winter evenings.

Opposite there stands a bookcase, with two shelves of books on bowls, from *Touchers and Rubs* to *End to End*. Uncle Fred has been saying for years that he is going to write a book about the game, but he has never got down to it. The most he has done is to ponder some titles. *Uncle Fred in the Springtime* would have been nice, if P. G. Wodehouse, Uncle Fred's favourite author, had not used it already. *The Wit and Wisdom of Uncle Fred* he ruled out as pretentious. *Thoughts of a Veteran Bowler* is the most suitable he has come up with so far.

In the kitchen there hangs a tea-towel decorated with amusing drawings and these printed cautions to bowlers: Don't allow your eyes to wander, Don't fire unless you have studied the head, Don't let your opponent rattle you, Don't green your woods narrow, Don't run off the mat when delivering, Don't let your opponent dictate the pace, Don't throw the jack, Don't be hasty in deciding which shot to play, Don't be distracted by shadows or movements, Don't relax when in the lead. Uncle Fred says that washing-up is a pleasure when you can simultaneously read such profound advice.

*       *       *

Uncle Fred's wife, Olga, does not dislike bowls: she's indifferent to it, that's all. When she married him she knew there would be no escape from the game and resigned herself to the fact. She has had the occasional roll-up, without the bug, as Uncle Fred inelegantly puts it, biting, and she quite enjoys snoozing in a deckchair beside the green on a sunny afternoon while her husband is in action. But these are the only concessions she has made or ever will make.

Their son Percy, so named, because he was born on the day Percy Baker won one of his EBA singles championships, plays a bit too, well enough to have won the club pairs with his father. He, however, much prefers snooker, which to Uncle Fred is tantamount to preferring a penny to a pound. They used to argue about it but then, realising how futile that was, withdrew, like battle-weary troops, to entrenched positions.

Uncle Fred is at best tolerant towards other games. He had a mathematics teacher at school who would refer to "inferior subjects such as English and religious education". That sums up Uncle Fred's attitude to soccer, cricket, and the rest. He has of course played them but, on mature reflection, considers them inferior to bowls as a lifelong provider of sporting satisfaction.

He's not backward in saying so, either. Many's the ding-dong he's had of an evening in the clubhouse, after a match, comparing one sport with another. Deep down he knows, from his old arguments with Percy, that these comparisons are silly and irrelevant. But he can't resist them. They're his love of bowls coming out, you see. People respect him for it, as they respect anybody with sincere opinions on a subject that, despite outward differences, unites them.

A closet sentimentalist, Uncle Fred – and a realist. Not even the coming of professionalism to the game has altered his perception of it. "Professionals?" he'd say. "They're nothing to do with us. They're up there" (gesturing to the heavens with his pipe and his pint). "We're the grass roots; the bedrock. The game existed for centuries without professionals. It wouldn't have lasted a week without trundlers like us."

A pause, to refill pipe and pint. Then: "Don't misunderstand me. I don't object to the money. I won a tenner in a tournament at Littlehampton once. It all went on shoes and Grippo."

*    *    *

Uncle Fred doesn't believe in coaching. He says that all the new bowler needs is to spend his first day or two on the green being shown the rudiments, and after that he can be left to fend for himself, seeking advice only when he wants it. "Trial and error," Uncle Fred intones, "trial and error. It's the only way to learn anything, from bowls to cooking. If the novice has got ball sense, that's half the battle. If he hasn't, common sense will do just as well, though the learning may take a little longer."

He remembers his own first day on the green as if it were

last week. "My father stood me on the mat, put a bowl in my hand, checked my grip, explained the relationship of the rings to the bias, told me to aim a yard to the right of the jack – and what did I do? I bowled a dead-length toucher with the first bowl of my life. It was a full-length jack, too."

When asked, as he invariably is, whether perhaps that was due to pure luck, he replies, with a straight face: "It might have been." And when further asked what happened to his next bowl, he says: "That first bowl was such a revelation to me that I've forgotten where the second one finished. But I like to think it was pretty close, a yard through, maybe, as insurance. Anyway, I haven't looked back since, though I say it myself."

His father occasionally discussed the game in terms of geometry, with imaginary lines drawn from mat to shoulder of green to jack, and so on. But that was as abstract as he ever got in his approach. "He told me to keep it simple, and draw, draw, and draw again," Uncle Fred says. "Fifty per cent of the game is in the delivery, the technique. The other fifty per cent is instinct, feel. When the two are harmonising, you're David Bryant. When they're not, you're a duffer."

Uncle Fred has a way with words and it's been suggested to him that he should write a book for beginners. "I told you, I don't believe in a lot of coaching," is his impatient response. "What I tell beginners wouldn't fill two pages. Besides, there are plenty of coaching books for those that want them – too many, in fact. I dipped into some of them a long time ago, but found that as soon as I got on the green everything I'd read went clean out of my head."

\*     \*     \*

Above Uncle Fred's desk there is a faded photograph taken during his early years in the club. It shows some of the afternoon "regulars" – those who could be relied upon, most days, for a roll-up. All lived near the green and all were in the habit of calling one another in the morning to find out who would be able to play after lunch. Fred (he was not Uncle yet) was welcomed into their company, and he has never forgotten them, or ceased to be grateful to them, for teaching him, unconsciously, things about the game not mentioned in books.

There stands Leslie, known to everyone as "Tod", a child-hood nickname derived from "toddler." He was a plump, shy man who always wore a white cap and, from a fixed stance, leaned sideways in a curious manner to deliver his bowls left-handed. He had lived in the same house, man and boy, for seventy years until, marrying late in life, he was persuaded by his wife, the stronger character of the two, to move to Cornwall. There he died within twelve months – of, it was suggested, a broken heart, for he had not wanted the uprooting.

Next to him in the photograph is Fred, not Uncle but another of that patronymic . He was of medium height but very broad, a generous extrovert, retired from the City, with a bass voice that dived into his boots and, such was its power, did the work of two in his choir. A colour drawing of him as Gilbert and Sullivan's Pirate King hung on his living-room wall. He was a fighter by nature, proud of having once, when far down in a final, given himself a pep-talk on the mat and gone on to win.

George is there, too, with his Italian wife; for both it was a second marriage, and a union of opposites, since he was as phlegmatic as she was excitable. George had been a prisoner-of-war in Germany but rarely talked of his experiences. Jack is in the foreground, wearing a cricket club sweater and keeping half an eye on his boxer dog, which used to watch the bowls peaceably enough from the expanse of grass in front of the pavilion. Not there are Tom and Lew and Frank and Charles and Harry; Lew once quoted Kipling at an AGM, a fairly unusual occurrence. They are all dead now, but still live in a portrait gallery in Uncle Fred's mind.

The sun was shining in that photograph, and when Uncle Fred recalls those distant afternoons, he has the illusion that it was always so.

\*     \*     \*

I don't think I've told you how Uncle Fred met his wife, Olga. It was at a cricket match. She was serving teas while her father umpired, and Uncle Fred first saw her through the steam from the urn. They were married eighteen months later and spent their honeymoon at Torquay during the open tournament, in which Uncle Fred lost in the semi-finals of the singles. He has since been heard to remark that if he couldn't win the singles as a bridegroom he'd have no chance at all of winning it as a husband and father – inscrutable logic, entirely typical of Uncle Fred. He's competed at Torquay for years now without getting to the final.

Olga's father was as obsessive about cricket as Uncle Fred is about bowls. Each man did his best to convert the other, with limited success; the most they achieved was grudging mutual respect, born, on Olga's father's side, of the discovery that W. G. Grace was an historic influence in both games.

Olga's father owned a complete set of Wisdens and Uncle Fred a complete set of EBA *Yearbooks*, but after the usual expressions of polite interest neither went near the other's shelves. One year Olga's father would take Uncle Fred to Lord's; the next, Uncle Fred would take Olga's father to Mortlake. And so it went on, until Olga's father died, rather suddenly, and Uncle Fred realised how much he missed him. The cross-fertilisation had been good for both these men of sport.

As to the relationship between Olga's father and Uncle Fred's father – but no, I mustn't entangle myself in family trees. The parents of Uncle Fred and Olga are dead, and Uncle Fred is the central figure in this narrative. It is sufficient to say that he and Olga are well matched after their fashion, like most couples. If they were not, they would scarcely have stayed together as long as they have. Uncle Fred eats, drinks, and sleeps bowls. His wife keeps the balance by turning a blind eye to it for much of the time. She is the neutral power, averting conflict.

Percy, their son, flits into and out of their lives, bowling a little, snookering much more, "doing his own thing", as sons do. They wonder if he will marry, and who. There was the daughter of a club member on the horizon, but she turned out to be a keen bowler, too keen for Percy's taste, and nothing came of it. He probably equates regular bowling with the regular life – in other words with "settling down" – and, being an individualist, he wants no truck with that for the moment.

*          *          *

Uncle Fred counts among the highlights of any year his first glimpse of outdoor play. It need not be at his own club. He might be travelling somewhere by train, at the beginning of May or even at the end of April, when he sees a neat green square with casually dressed figures on it, moving among bowls too scattered to be described as a head.

That gives him a sense of well-being, as if he had come home, or had suddenly remembered something of great private importance. It marks the true beginning of his year, for Uncle Fred cares little for the indoor game, and tends to hibernate during the cold months, calling himself a bit of a hedgehog. Indoor stadiums can resemble crematoriums from the outside, not to be compared with the old wooden pavilion, perhaps with a verandah, seen from the train.

Next day may find Uncle Fred at his club, performing one of his first tasks of the season – pinning up a list of members willing to mark. The list was his idea, a few years back. For too long those wanting a marker had often had no option but to ring round on the off chance, sometimes, in an emergency, approaching people they scarcely knew. The list brought order to the whole business, and you can guess whose name is always the first on it. Uncle Fred enjoys marking, saying it's the next best thing to playing, and that the abler players usually make the best markers.

Impartiality should of course be taken for granted in a marker, but there can be embarrassments, and Uncle Fred tells of an experience of his own in an early round of a county singles, with a novice marker he had had to engage at the last moment. He was bowling badly, against a moderate opponent, and at the conclusion of yet another losing end the marker said, audibly enough: "Come on, Fred, this isn't like you." His opponent tactfully showed no annoyance, merely observing, with a thin smile, that it was obvious which man the marker wanted to win, or words to that effect. Uncle Fred told the marker, as soon as he could, to keep his views to himself: and never engaged him again.

He also tells of another marker who, on being asked which was shot bowl, pointed to it and then, sticking out an arm, said: "And this is your best hand to come." But that was different: that was funny.

*       *       *

"One of the great things about bowls is that it doesn't pretend to be something it isn't. It hasn't got delusions of grandeur. I mean, if you listen to the soccer people, you would think their game is fantastic and wonderful and the most exciting in the world. But do you know, I think it's dull, skilful but dull, and I'm able to say that because I've played it a bit, on sufferance, at school and in the army, and I've tried hard to see what everyone raves about. For the life of me I can't. To me it's just a dull game. All that tip-tapping for fewer and fewer goals. Look at the World Cup. Pavarotti was the only star."

That's Uncle Fred astride one of his hobby-horses. If you remind him that soccer and bowls are incompatible, he'll agree with you and then, like a soap-box orator, repeat his original assertion.

"Don't misunderstand me," he goes on "bowls has its faults. I can see them as clearly as anybody. The critics say it's so boring it's like watching peas soak. They wouldn't say that if they understood it. It's a slow-burn game. That's its character. Every game has its own character. Some have got action, some have got tension, suspense. Bowls has got suspense."

"Alfred Hitchcock should have been a bowler – perhaps he was. Remember that film when he slipped in and out of a scene lugging a cello? I can imagine him doing the same wearing a blazer and carrying a bowls bag. Probably there'd be a firearm in the bag."

"No. The main fault with bowls, in my humble opinion, is that there's too much bull, especially over dress. Let's be smart, by all means, but not to the extent of being tailor's dummies. Take the fuss about ties. On a scorching day, in a club friendly – a club friendly, mark you – there has to be some pompous ass who likes to come forward and announce, as if he were doing everyone a big favour, that ties may be removed. Thank you very much. It always surprises me that grown men wait to be told. If it's as hot as all that, ties should never have been worn in the first instance."

Such sentiments may appear strange, coming from an ex-regimental sergeant-major. But Uncle Fred says he was never one for undue spit and polish. He wouldn't dream of having the rink strings painted white.

*          *          *

Uncle Fred looks on holidays as gratuitous interruptions of the season and tries to avoid them whenever possible. "With all that bowling," Olga says, "your life's one long holiday." "I don't need to go away, then, do I?" he retorts. "Well, I do, and I'm not going without you," Olga says with finality; and off they go, Uncle Fred making sure to stow his bowls gear in the car boot.

You know how you often read of people stopping to watch

a village cricket match over the gate; perhaps even being offered a game if one team is a man short, or asked to umpire. Uncle Fred will tell you corresponding tales about bowls. Out walking in the Cotswolds, he has happened – deliberate accident – to pass the local green, paused to study form, and in next to no time been invited to join in. "Have you played this game before?" they may ask, and Uncle Fred, bent over his shoelaces, smiles. One thing leads to another, and he could finish up playing as often on holiday as he does at home: which neither surprises nor displeases Olga, who would rather see him bowling and happy than not bowling and morose. Besides, she reasons that, whatever Uncle Fred is doing, she is still getting her deserved rest from domestic routine.

He, it should be said, is an EBA man through and through. He has spent holidays in Federation country but never played that code; the only crown green he has seen was at Preston, where there was one opposite his hotel; and the idea of playing on dust or gravel, as in boules, depresses him, for green, he says, is the true colour of the game and always will be.

Back from holiday, he assures everybody that he had enjoyed himself, having by way of a change played a lot of bowls, and then starts catching up with his competitions, noting that his next opponent in the championship is a new member, recently joined from another club, who is already shunned by many as a bore because he never stops talking about the game. They've dubbed him The Long-Playing Record.

Post-mortems are one thing; monologues quite another. This man's exposition of the forehand and backhand peculiarities of any rink on the green would baffle Einstein, provided it didn't send him to sleep first. Listening, or trying not to listen while appearing to take a polite interest, you realise why he and his previous club parted company. And

I can now tell you that Uncle Fred beat him, and bought him a drink afterwards, but went home before the slow-motion replay could begin.

*     *     *

One of Uncle Fred's boasts is that, in the course of his long career, he has qualified for the EBA championships at Paddington, Mortlake, and Worthing. He went out in the first round each time and doesn't mind admitting it. "The thing is, I got there," he says. "It's like Everest. I never stood on the summit but I did reach base camp. That's worth putting on anybody's c.v."

He can remember, at Mortlake, meeting, though not playing, Percy Baker. He also remembers Algy Allen, Tom Fleming, and Charlie Mercer. In 1973, the last year of the nationals at Mortlake, he qualified in the fours, then stayed on and saw David Bryant beat Ian Harvey in the singles final – DJB's third win running in that championship. "I saw history made," Uncle Fred says.

He played third man in the fours, his favourite position, a fact that might surprise those who, knowing his assertiveness as well as his skill, see him as a natural skip. "I never object to being told what to do," he assures the sceptics, "provided I respect the man telling me." He is scornful of the idea that one position is more important than another in a rink. "They're all important, of course they are. You hear so-called experts belittling the No. 2. Moonshine. It's a team game and with only four men there's nowhere for anybody to hide. If one man's having an off day the four will be very lucky to win, if the opposition are any good."

Uncle Fred still pays occasional visits to Worthing as a spectator, always staying in the same guest house, just off the Brighton road, a short step from Beach House Park. He prefers Worthing to Paddington and Mortlake because he enjoys the seaside; and on a fine evening he can often be found walking the front between the aquarena and the yacht club. That's quite a hike but Uncle Fred is nothing if not fit for his age, and rarely pauses for a breather.

One year he recalled reading in the local paper that a man, a tramp down from London, had been found dead, suspected murdered, in one of the beach shelters. Not the sort of happening you connect with Worthing, and as such it makes an anecdote for Uncle Fred during long winter evenings in the clubhouse.

\*       \*       \*

George Scadgell regarded open and seaside tournaments as the finest entertainment in the game, and Uncle Fred agrees. Uncle Fred no longer enters for them, mainly on account of *anno domini*, but enjoys reflecting on the many years when he did, and urging the younger men to try their luck.

"Don't be so parish-pump," he will say if they demur. "Forget the club for a week. Bowl somewhere else, meet different players, it's invaluable experience and a great holiday." "But the wife . . . ", they may say. "Take her with you," is the retort. "She'll enjoy it, too." More often than not, they do and she does; and from then on, year after year, they return to Eastbourne or Cromer, Hastings or Teignmouth, eagerly filling in entry forms during a tournament to make sure of their places twelve months hence.

Uncle Fred has played at Eastbourne, Worthing, Bournemouth, and Rock Park, in Barnstaple, among others. He was only once at Rock Park, and that was when there had been no rain in the region for six weeks, and the green was a uniform brown; it was like bowling on sand. Uncle Fred loves to study the honours boards at every club he visits, famous or obscure, and he noted that Rock Park had produced an EBA singles finalist, C. J. Webber.

Not least does he remember Barnstaple for the excellent restaurant, run by a bearded German, where he and Olga dined. One evening they overheard a child at the table behind them pipe up: "This is better than school dinners." Uncle Fred and Olga thought it better than the Savoy, although their knowledge of the latter establishment was strictly limited, and gratefully signed the visitors' book, noting Jeremy Thorpe among the celebrities who had preceded them.

Bournemouth was the best of the best for quality of greens, Uncle Fred having fond memories of, in particular, Boscombe Cliff and Swanmore Gardens, with its frame of rose bushes. The Princes Park greens at Eastbourne were scarcely inferior then to those of Bournemouth; some respected drawing bowlers say they are now superior. These are subjective opinions, however, frequently dependent on whether a man has won or lost.

The last time Uncle Fred competed at Worthing, he advanced in the triples at Tarring Priory, in a match played throughout in rain, which dripping trees made worse, but lost on the same green the next morning. One year, playing with two strangers, he found himself up against Peter Line in the consolation triples at Beach House Park – a good example of the egalitarianism of these tournaments. He has been to Worthing oftener than to any of the others, so often that he believes he could now find his way round it blindfolded, and write an accurate and comprehensive guide to its eating-places, starting, on the western edge, with the Sea Lane Cafe – "Not yet world famous; Still open eight days a week; Nine-day licence applied for."

Happy days.

\*          \*          \*

Many men of Uncle Fred's generation used to be against women bowlers on principle, though what that principle was none could say exactly. Uncle Fred, more far-sighted, and a romantic at heart, supported women bowlers in his club from the outset, and was unpopular with the committee as a result. Now, women bowlers are the norm almost everywhere, and the mixed game flourishes.

Which gives Uncle Fred the cue to suggest official international matches between mixed rinks, two men and two
women in each. He'd like to see, for example, David Bryant
as skip with Norma Shaw his No. 3, or Wynne Richards
third to Mary Price. Uncle Fred believes that a British Isles
mixed team championship at the same time of year as the
late lamented Masters tournament would fill Beach House
Park.

He himself has played a lot of mixed bowls but only once
or twice with his wife. That was in the early days when it
seemed the obvious thing to do; but it didn't work, partly
perhaps because Olga was insufficiently interested, more
likely because husband and wife partnerships often fail to
"click" on the green. Temperament, ever unpredictable, could
be one factor. Another could be the subtle shift in authority:
if one partner is accustomed to ruling the roost at home, he,
or she, may, without entirely realising it, resent having to
accept instructions and advice on the green, however well
conveyed.

Anyway, Uncle Fred, after an interval, asked Jane, who
was some years younger, to join him in the club's mixed
pairs, and they won it in their second season together. Jane
was an inexperienced player but a steady, unflappable lead,
and she instinctively understood Uncle Fred and knew how
to humour him – which was half the battle. She didn't take the
game too seriously, and that also helped. They entered for the
national mixed pairs in its first year and lost in a preliminary
round, on their own green on a grey Saturday afternoon, when
the club had an away match; their voices made echoes in the
deserted place.

Women bowlers' white uniform, strictly regulated at
county and national level, continues to excite derision.
Uncle Fred used to dislike it but he has come round
to the opinion expressed by George Burrows: "Experience
has proved that their distinguishing county colours, made

very effective in their hatbands, provide quite sufficient variation of colour . . . Elegant as were the flowing skirts and floral or feathered hats of the women who started the game in 1908, they were pre-eminently unsuitable for serious bowls, and the regulation costume has everything to recommend it."

*       *       *

The only limerick about bowls that Uncle Fred has ever seen in print ran as follows:

> At Plymouth Drake bowled on the Hoe
> He said "I'm left-handed, you know."
> His sinister woods
> Delivered the goods
> As he cackhandedly finished the foe.

Uncle Fred thought so little of it, particularly the clumsy last line, that he sat down and tried to write some limericks of his own. He eschewed Drake as an overworked subject in any case, and eventually, after creative wrestlings, came up with these specimens:

> There was a young bowler named Lucky
> Whose mother conceived in Kentucky;
> When he took up the game
> But failed to find fame,
> He decided Kentucky's unlucky.

> Let me tell you the tale of Joe Barker
> Who wanted to be a great marker.
> With his measure and chalk
> And constable's walk,
> Oh, how they made fun of Joe Barker.

> There was a girl bowler called Pat
> Who was never seen wearing a hat,

Till up jumped her captain
And cried "Put your hat on!
"Without it you're nude on the mat."

Not brilliant, Uncle Fred thought, but on the other hand
not bad for a beginner. The one about the girl was the best,
in his modest opinion. He sent them to the local rag, which
returned them "with regret". "Regret!" he exclaimed to his
wife. "Rubbish! They could've saved themselves the regret by
publishing the things. I've seen much worse."

Still, he was not too disappointed, or surprised. He has, as
you know, been the club's press officer in his time, and a
conscientious one, too. It was an experience that hardened
him to rejection. How often he had supplied information that
never appeared.

It's the same in all the papers, he says. Bowls is the poor
relation among sports. If you can find a couple of paragraphs
about it at the foot of a page, you're doing well. He consoles
himself with the thought that in the end it doesn't really
matter. The game's the thing. And with that he turns to the
far more urgent business of polishing his woods for his singles
match in the evening.

*       *       *

Nothing tickles Uncle Fred more than the habit among bowlers of blaming the green when they lose. It was difficult. It
was impossible. It was diabolical. Should never have been
used for a competition. Ought to be reported to the county.
Like playing on a ploughed field. Don't mind taking the rough
with the smooth, but when it's all rough . . .

"The one thing they hardly ever do," Uncle Fred says, "is
blame themselves. If a chap says he couldn't find it, and
leaves it at that, he's saying all that needs to be said. No use
blaming the rink or the green. They're there to be overcome,
like wickets. Complaining won't alter the scoreboard. Best just
to forget it and go home to the missus.

"I once knew a chap, a very good bowler, who was white-washed 21–0 in a county singles. Do you know what he said afterwards? He said, 'Charlie was 21 shots better than me on the day.' Next season he happened to be drawn against the same man in the same competition, and played him on the same green, and won by a street. Funny, isn't it?

"I'm a great believer in the sub-conscious element in this game. You don't always lose because you play badly. You can lose because you got out of bed on the wrong side, or you're overdrawn at the bank, or your daughter's engagement's been broken off, or the steak you had at supper was like old leather, or you were caught in the rush-hour.

"They talk a lot about preparing mentally for an important match, relaxing, getting there in good time, having a quiet cup of coffee, and so forth. It doesn't always follow. It's possible to be too relaxed. I've sometimes been up to town and arrived back at the club at the very last moment, and gone out and played a blinder. All the dashing around can relax you in a way, putting the match out of your mind, so that you don't worry about it.

"What's that you're asking? Who was the man who was whitewashed? It was years ago but I remember it was yours truly. It was an education, I can tell you. You're not an experienced bowler until you've been whitewashed. I was lucky to get nil.

"And now, after all that, if you want my advice about the best attitude to bad greens, and how to approach big matches, I would say, 'Do it your way, like Mr Sinatra.'"

\*     \*     \*

There is a television set in Uncle Fred's house but not where you'd expect. Most people have theirs in the living-room, crouched in a corner, a predator ready to pounce on the attention. Uncle Fred has his in a little spare room at the back and, when bowls is on, that is where he withdraws, leaving Olga to her own devices, which definitely don't include sport.

Bowls is one of the few programmes Uncle Fred deigns to watch on the box. He's not all that keen on the indoor game and says that he watches not so much for the bowling as for the close-ups of the players' faces. He considers himself a bit of a psychologist and reckons he can tell far in advance who is going to win just from studying the eyes. He's into body language, too, being himself a graphic exponent of it on the green; he's often been called the local Harry Reston. Age restricts his contortions these days, but in moments of high excitement he can still forget it and turn ballet dancer.

Like any self-respecting bowler, Uncle Fred is sorry to see the time allotted to bowls on TV being cut and cut and cut. He wrote to the television people about it but they didn't reply. "No manners", Uncle Fred snorts. But he knows the game will survive and he's inspired by that. He sees this as a passing phase, the game touching a peak of popularity on TV in the Eighties, and now falling away, perhaps to disappear from the small screen well before the turn of the century.

"I'll probably have pegged out by then," he says, winking. "Gone to the Great Bowling Green in the Sky. Thank goodness they don't have TV there. If they did, I wouldn't go. No, I don't think the ordinary bowler will miss bowls when it's not on TV any more. He'll just watch more football instead – after he's played his handicap singles; a true bowler always has his priorities right."

As I said, Uncle Fred doesn't watch much TV. Soap operas he cannot abide, chat shows he regards as inferior to bowling club conversations, and comedy he dismisses as moronic. If it were not for oddments of sport, the occasional play, and his wife's favourites, he'd chuck the set away. The first bowls he saw on it was John Dunn beating David Bryant in a world championship. "Better than *The Sound of Music*", Uncle Fred murmurs.

*    *    *

Uncle Fred is sociable enough, to the extent of rarely being at a loss for a word to anyone who cares to listen; but the social side of his club, although he knows its value, interests him little. They once pressed him into being the chairman of the social committee, but as soon as his term was up he was glad to resign, leaving tombola and dancing to those who care for such pursuits. At heart he's a bowling man, first, last and always, his eye constantly straying to the green even on the wettest day, his fingers itching for the curve of the bowl, the whole of him wanting the stimulus and tension of competitive play.

There was, however, one social occasion, only one, when he appeared in a very different, and unexpected, light: when, in spite of himself, the dedicated bowler gave way to a music-hall performer. It occurred, many years ago, during a club tour to Ilfracombe. On the last night it was suggested that as many as possible did a turn, whatever they liked (within respectable limits, of course), and no shirking. Some sang, some played the piano, some recited, some danced, some told stories, some clowned.

Uncle Fred happened to be last on, and he sang "Get Me to the Church on Time" from *My Fair Lady*, which brought down the house, or rather hotel, with the entire company agreeing that Stanley Holloway had a worthy rival as Doolittle, and Olga, Uncle Fred's wife, shedding tears of delight and saying that her Fred had missed his vocation. So Uncle Fred, responding to the clamour for an encore, sang "Get Me to the Church" again, and if they had been in a theatre he would have continued singing, but the hour was late, and after a short closing speech – by Uncle Fred, who else? – and "Auld Lang Syne", the lights went out all over Ilfracombe.

Uncle Fred has not sung in public since. "I keep it for my bath," he says, with perhaps surprising diffidence. Did he miss his vocation, as Olga claimed? "Definitely not. Being able to sing well isn't too unusual. It's being a Caruso that's unusual. Anyway, Doolittle's song is more speaking than singing."

Singing is one of Uncle Fred's private methods of staying healthy. He's seen so many bowlers grow fat and wheezy, and being a singer, and only an occasional pipe-smoker off the green, nowhere else, has helped him avoid that fate. He prides himself on enjoying everything about a game of bowls, scenery and birdsong included, and says it's impossible to do that through a perpetual cloud of smoke.

*       *       *

Not many can say now that they have played on the old outdoor green at Alexandra Palace, but Uncle Fred can. That was in the Fifties, before the club, and the adjacent racecourse, closed down. The green was cut out of the hill by German prisoners during the First World War. In the Palace building itself, above the BBC, there is a tiny indoor club, probably the highest in the land, and Uncle Fred has bowled there too; and never forgotten the awesome spectacle of London presented from the terrace. Everywhere you look, London: Middlesex, Hertfordshire, Essex, Surrey, Kent – all there, if not visible, with the sounds of millions reduced to a murmur. Far below, the trains, the toy trains, slide into and out of King's Cross.

Uncle Fred is a "collector" of clubs in distinctive places. He has been ferried across the Thames to the Island Bohemian at Reading; stopped to watch Concorde passing over the Royal Household at Windsor; skipped on the City of London green; and seen the Yeoman Warders in action, corner to corner, on their oblong lawn at the Tower.

What he cannot say, much though he'd like to, is that his own club is distinctive in either position or appearance. It is like a hundred – a thousand – others, better than some, not so well endowed as a few. You could take a photograph of it and say, "There's a typical English bowling club." A green of forty yards, the clubhouse along one side, tall hedges abutting on private gardens, seats dedicated to worthy club servants of the past. School-children sometimes throw things over the hedges and call out satirical remarks.

At one corner of the green is the only unusual feature – an old-fashioned lamp-post; why or when it came to be there, and to remain there, nobody knows. It is never lit, of course, although there have been suggestions that it should be, when competitions, notoriously the handicap singles, drag on into darkness. Uncle Fred remembers finishing a singles by light reflected from the pavilion. He would have won, he says, if the shadows hadn't made him misjudge his length and fall a yard short with his last bowl.

The lamp-post, by the way, reminds Uncle Fred of the City of London club, where they have an old drinking-fountain at a corner of the green. But there is no bandstand at his club, as there is at the City of London, and the Queen doesn't go by, as she occasionally does at the Royal Household. The mayor of the borough is the best that Uncle Fred's club can show in the way of distinguished visitors, and that was a while ago, when they had their golden jubilee. Perhaps they'll splash out for their centenary and invite Whatsisname – you know, the famous bowler.

*      *      *

Uncle Fred has thought of entering for Mastermind, with his specialised subject bowls from 5000 BC, or whenever, to the present day. He says a more exact title for the programme would be Mastermemory, and on that premise believes he would have a good chance, his memory for bowls being second to none. Percy Baker remembered individual heads in matches played long ago, and on his humbler level Uncle Fred also aspires to total recall.

One of the few things he does have difficulty in remembering is the location of certain clubs. In his early years, when he couldn't afford a car, he went on foot or by public transport, and sometimes walked in circles for half an hour or longer, asking one stranger after another for directions, before reaching journey's end. When eventually he did get a car, it was much the same story, with the extra problem of parking.

The point is that too many bowling clubs are signposted inadequately or not at all. The worst offenders are down alleyways between private houses. If there is no signpost, you can pass and repass the alleyway and never notice it. During a leisurely ramble it is a charming experience to come on a bowling club tucked away out of sight, which you didn't know existed; but if you are due to play a match there and can't find it, charming is not the word.

Uncle Fred says the game is far too modest about itself and cites this elementary yet important matter of signposting, or lack of it, as an example. And if that is bad, what can be said of towns which host national and international championships and do nothing to publicise them – not even putting up appropriate road signs? Uncle Fred in his indignation would like to – but let us, for once, place a kindly hand over Uncle Fred's mouth, things are getting too serious. Instead, let us return to Mastermind, or Mastermemory, and imagine our hero in the black leather chair.

He says he could take the pressure and wouldn't "freeze". As it happens, he knows a lady who failed in the final because she hadn't eaten properly all day and, moreover, had drunk sherry beforehand that clouded her senses. In her normal form she would have won. Uncle Fred would avoid these mistakes and be ready and able for questions such as "Where was bowls first played in the southern hemisphere?", "London's first public green was laid down in which of these parks – Hyde Park, Battersea Park or Regent's Park?" and "Who was the first man to win the EBA singles twice?"

"Yes, Fred, I know you're a walking encyclopaedia on bowls, but what about the general knowledge questions?" you'd be entitled to ask him. "I'd be confident," he'd reply. "I've read a lot of books on a lot of subjects, and like all good bowlers I read the *Telegraph*, so I'm not a complete ignoramus. Why, even if that fellow Magnusson asked me about other

games, I might surprise a few people. I could tell him a thing
or two about lacrosse."

*          *          *

Uncle Fred prefers, as he puts it, to travel light on the
green. Not for him the impedimenta that some bowlers lug
around while playing. He even removes his wristwatch and
empties his pockets of money, ignoring comments that he
risks having them stolen by leaving them in his jacket in the
changing-room, home or away. He's done this for years and
lost nothing, and he'll go on doing it – go on trusting in the
innate honesty of the bowling race.

He long ago gave up using a drying-cloth. On wet days he
found that when he wiped his bowls, imparting an artificial
sheen, they were more difficult to control than if he left the
moisture and grass on them. By slightly adjusting the position
of his fingers, moving the thumb farther across the top of
the bowl, he obtained all the control he needed. He has met
bowlers who do the same, though not many.

A measure he cannot entirely avoid carrying. If he's playing
third, it is not right always to be borrowing someone else's,
and if he's marking it's essential. At all other times the
measure stays in his locker.

Yet, as he's quick to point out, a lot of bowlers take a
drying-cloth and a measure with them everywhere, whether
needed or not, almost like status symbols. "They probably
sleep with them under the pillow," he cackles. The measure
is usually one of the new-fangled type that clips to the belt
or waistband, and the drying-cloth hangs from a pocket like
a shirt-tail. Ultimate absurdity, you even see cloths flaunted
like that indoors.

"Believe it or not," the perennial cloth-carriers tell Uncle
Fred, "the cloth helps us to concentrate between deliveries.
Wiping the bowl has a sort of calming effect. It's only a habit,
you see." Uncle Fred does see: but it still amuses him, just as
his habit of shedding wristwatch and cash amuses others.

Also amusing to him – and these, too, are habits – are two of the gestures made by the more fretful skips. One is when a bowl is obviously too heavy, the other when it's going to stop short. In the first case the skip makes violent downward motions with both hands; in the second, he makes straining movements towards his chest. Every bowler will know what Uncle Fred means, but not every bowler will see the resemblances that he sees.

"It's the Tchaikovsky piano concerto," he says of the first; and of the second: "It's Boat Race time."

\*        \*        \*

Uncle Fred's club, in common with many another, has had difficulty sometimes in finding enough players for matches. The situation became so serious a few years ago that the committee ruled that anybody not putting his name down for at least ten matches would be excluded from all club competitions the following season.

"Blackmail," some members cried. "What else could we do?" the captain said. "We can't keep cancelling matches because we couldn't raise a team. We'd lose the fixtures, and goodwill, and get a bad reputation. Something drastic had to be done." Uncle Fred, as a born competitor, was never too keen on club friendlies, but he saw both sides of the case, and supported the committee's action, while sympathising with the "blackmail" argument.

A season or two later, with the membership up, the situation righted itself, and the committee revoked its ruling. Now, finding players is not the problem. The problem is spreading selection fairly among all those who put their names down: an insoluble problem, as it happens, given the readiness of certain members (every club has them) to moan at the slightest affront, real or imagined, probably the latter. Two of them resigned, saying they were never chosen and alleging prejudice, but were soon replaced by younger men, less experienced but more flexible.

There is a waiting-list now, and that means regular interviews of aspiring members. These interviews are conducted
in the changing-room by a panel of three – the captain, the
secretary, and Uncle Fred. As a rule, Uncle Fred does most
of the talking, and he claims to be able to spot an unsuitable
candidate – what he calls "a wrong 'un" or "a rotten apple" –
within the opening two minutes. If asked how he can tell, he
replies: "I feel it in my bones."

Only once has his judgment been at fault. A man who had
belonged to several other local clubs in the past was admitted
as a member, and was soon found with his hand in the till.
"That taught me a lesson," Uncle Fred admits. "Always be
suspicious of anybody who has belonged to a lot of other
clubs. If there wasn't something odd about him, he wouldn't
have left them all."

Uncle Fred is, as you know, a one-club man, a perfect
example of the type, a believer in continuity and stability. He
is almost as much married to the club as he is to Olga – more
so, Olga says in moments of irritation. He has provided for the
club in his will, and likes to think, without boastfulness, that
after he starts "pushing up daisies", as he habitually terms it,
he will be remembered for a very long time indeed. There is,
in fact, though he has not been told yet, a plan to name the
club gates after him. You can be sure he would love that.

*     *     *

As I've said before, Uncle Fred has a take-it-or-leave-it attitude
to the indoor game: mainly leave it, he himself would add,
waving his pipe and his pint. So when somebody at his
club suggested introducing a system of ranking points for
the bowling members, Uncle Fred was dismissive.

"That may be alright for inferior games like snooker and
tennis," he said, "but it's not fitting for bowls." Mr Somebody,
who perhaps had been reading the newspapers too much, was
not to be put off. "I couldn't agree less," he bravely returned.
"If they can have a ranking system for Bryant and Allcock

indoors, there's no logical reason why we shouldn't have one of our own for Smith and Jones outdoors. It would be fun, add to the interest, give everyone a bit extra to play for."

Mr Somebody raised the idea again at the annual meeting but it was rejected, by a large majority, after a speech by Uncle Fred in which he condemned ranking points as an instrument of professionalism and said they were spurious, based as they were on statistics, which as all the world knew could be manipulated to prove anything. "What's the use of being ranked No. 1," he asked in his peroration, "if No. 100 comes along and beats you out of sight?"

A few sided with Mr Somebody, considering that Uncle Fred's rhetorical question, far from being an argument against a ranking system, was in fact, from one angle, the most convincing point in its favour. But the motion failed anyway, most of those present feeling that this was just another bandwagon and they had no wish to jump on it. Instinctively they followed Uncle Fred who, with all his faults, to them represented the best kind of traditionalist, a man not hide-bound but with a sure nose for the ephemeral and the pretentious.

After the meeting Uncle Fred and Mr Somebody, between whom there had always been great respect, had a drink together, and Mr Somebody asked Uncle Fred – just out of curiosity, nothing serious, mind you – where he thought he, Uncle Fred, would stand in a ranking system supposing one were introduced in the club. "No. 1, of course," was Uncle Fred's unhesitating answer: which he qualified by saying: "But if I was No. 100 I wouldn't mind. It's all nonsense, isn't it?" And, mellowing to suit the occasion, Mr Somebody echoed: "Yes, it's all nonsense. Couldn't agree more."

\*     \*     \*

There is a club, not far from Uncle Fred's, where it is stated in the rules, under the sensational sub-heading, Politics and Religion, that "No general discussion on these subjects shall be permitted." This has always puzzled Uncle Fred. "What else do you discuss?" he asks. "I mean, if you care to stretch a point, almost any subject comes into the category of politics or religion – even bowls. There's a lot of politics behind the scenes, and some players look on the game as a religion."

In this connection he recalls a green-keeper at his own club, in the dear dead days when they could afford one. This man was portly and cloth-capped, his name was Joe, and he was good at his job but garrulous, loudly so. He read everything, from newspapers to encyclopaedias, and liked to air the latest bit of knowledge he had acquired, sometimes standing on the bank to do it while a match was in progress.

Uncle Fred can't remember Joe discoursing on religion, but he had earfuls of science and biology, as well as astronomy, meteorology, military history, the trade union movement, steam trains (Joe loved travel) and the Kaiser. Uncle Fred doubts whether Joe retained this knowledge. As soon as he had ventilated it, he probably forgot most of it, in the excitement of some fresh discovery. "He had an inquiring mind, did Joe. I just wished he'd come down to earth and talk about bowls occasionally. But he didn't. I don't think he was very interested in sport – and him a green-keeper."

Joe lived in the next street to the club, with his wife and unmarried daughter. He and the club parted company when he asked for a second pay rise within eighteen months and was told he was being unreasonable and they couldn't afford it. After that they decided to do the green themselves, and have been doing it for nearly twenty years, apart from a couple of seasons when they hired contractors, who, more accustomed to public recreation grounds, cut the green but seemed never to have heard of tining, fertilising and scarifying.

Joe is dead now. Uncle Fred attended the funeral and as he sat in the sparsely filled chapel had a vision of Joe, had he been a mourner, gleaning things from the service, then going round to the club afterwards and expounding them to all and sundry from the bank.

*       *       *

Hooliganism on the green? It was unheard-of in Uncle Fred's younger days when bowls was the ultimate peaceful pastime and society was different. But nowhere is safe now.

Look at what happened at Uncle Fred's club quite recently, during an afternoon roll-up, men and women, the sun shining, birds singing, trees rustling, Mrs Bickerstaff getting the tea and biscuits ready, a job she's been doing for 20 years or more. Through the gate came four youths, shouting and swearing and throwing bottles and stones on to the green. The police were fetched to remove them; it turned out they had been in court that morning on drugs charges and, released on bail, had had a few drinks and gone looking vengefully for trouble.

It was a shock to the club's system: made the members wonder if it would happen again: made them look twice at innocent strangers passing beyond the hedge: made them doubly sympathetic when they heard of other clubs suffering in similar or worse ways – from nocturnal tramplings in football boots, from refuse sacks slit open and the contents strewn across the green, from broken windows, theft, aimless malice. Little could be done to prevent it; an ordinary club can't afford to have floodlights and guard dogs. In any case, as Uncle Fred pointed out, you can put up railings and fences and strengthen locks, but if these wretched people want to get in they'll get in. So you just have to live with the risks.

However, there have been no more unsavoury incidents at Uncle Fred's club. The invasion by the youths was too grotesque to recur, members told themselves, and thus far they've been right. Mild discord on the green, yes, but no hooliganism, nothing that quick reference to the laws of the game, or plain common sense, couldn't sort out.

*       *       *

Uncle Fred has a soft spot for a book called *Bowls – Light and Merry* (possibly printed privately) which Olga found second-hand in Lyme Regis. Inside there's an inscription by the author, Evan Llewellyn, to F. W. Piggins, Worthing Bowling Club, with the date July 1948. The original price was 3s 6d; Olga paid £2.80.

The book is a miscellany, without too much whimsy, and Llewellyn, described as late of West Streatham BC, London, now Worthing BC, writes in a foreword that it is not intended to instruct anyone in the game, although, as Uncle Fred discerned, you could learn quite a lot by reading between the lines. The theme is humour, with the note struck on the opening page:

> "Bowling calls for mild exercise of body, mental alertness in noting positions of woods, calculation, concentration and anticipation. A wonderful array of virtues these, but thank goodness the average bowler does not dwell overmuch upon them."

Now listen to Llewellyn on the four players in a rink:

> "I am the lead, but not the leader. I start, but am not always in at the finish. I am the first person singular of the rink, and there is no competition for my place . . . When I bowl the eloquence of the skip's hands is a thing to marvel at."

> The No. 2: "While waiting his turn he casually mentions to the opposing second that he's suffering from committeeitis: he's really a No. 3. In fact in his last club he was never earlier than No. 3. He wants to be an individualist and a law unto himself."

> The third: "This man . . . is the show boy of the rink and is the originator of the contortion and the mince. His lame left amble after the wood, his camel roll, his sudden dash, stop and corkscrew twist defy his imitators. His cup of movement and of ecstasy would be full were he

still allowed to hurdle up the bank and turn round."

And lastly:

> "Some skips are born for great things,
> Some skips are born for small,
> Of some 'tis not recorded
> Why they were born at all."

Llewellyn suggests Dunbolin, Upandown, Backwoods and Morelandia as names for bowlers' houses, and indulges in this flight of fancy on "ladybirds":

> "Ladies make a most attractive show on the green. Their presence reminds us of daisies on the lawn and their befitting dress and general daintiness add colour and charm to what is sometimes a dull setting. But cannot their pirouetting upon delivery of the wood and tripping down the rink be put to some more entertaining purpose; cannot they exhibit their natural charm and art and craft for the delectation of bankers and other rinkers? The green is a ready-made and natural stage for dancing and ballet."

*     *     *

Finding birthday and Christmas presents for Uncle Fred is never a problem. Just about anything to do with bowls will do; and he doesn't in the least mind duplication. If somebody gives him a measure, when he already has half a dozen, he's as grateful as if it were his first. Cards, too, are easy, or the birthday sort are, given that, despite the indoor game, bowls and Christmas don't quite go together.

Uncle Fred keeps all his cards, going back years and years. He was born in August – someone with his future simply had to enter the world at the height of the outdoor season – and one of his most recent birthday cards, showing a head of bowls, was captioned "The winning wood." He studied it for a while and then, with a frown, inquired, "But which *is* the winning wood?" Sure enough, when you looked more closely, and even allowing for a certain foreshortening, you could see there was very little between the nearest bowls. Only Uncle Fred would have noticed a detail like that.

"I'd put the tape on it," he said. "Don't believe in taking chances. Might even be a tied end." You felt that, if he had known the name and address of the artist, he would have written to him pointing out this technical flaw in an otherwise masterly piece of work.

So Uncle Fred has birthday and Christmas cards aplenty: but – and I make no apology for the *non sequitur* – no cigarette cards, although he was a collector when young, with complete sets of military uniforms and dogs and cars and trains and aircraft and film actors. Those being the days before bowls took over his life, he also had complete sets of sportsmen – but there wasn't a bowler among them. In retrospect Uncle Fred considers this a lamentable oversight on the part of the tobacco people. Were they dead to the virtues and traditions of the noble game? Had they never heard of Jimmy Carruthers, Irvine Watson, Percy Baker, Harold Webber, Bert Keech?

Nowadays, certainly, there'd be no excuse for leaving out bowlers, when you think of the fame of Bryant and Allcock. Indeed, men like Uncle Fred – in Uncle Fred's not entirely frivolous opinion – deserve to be on cigarette cards themselves. Uncle Fred says he's as important to bowls as any world champion, and would willingly pose for your archetypal bowler, almost like a soldier in those old sets of uniforms.

\*　　　　\*　　　　\*

When his enthusiasm for the game is at its height, Uncle Fred can't bear distractions of any kind. Take – or, as he would advise, don't take – those tedious suburban preoccupations, gardening, do-it-yourself, shopping, and travel. His attitudes to them tell us much about his character.

He enjoys looking at gardens, and naturally prefers flower beds to concrete, but apart from cutting the grass and doing a little weeding – "just to show willing" and to satisfy his tidy mind – he has no interest. When Olga in their early days chided him about it, suggesting that for all he knew he might have green fingers, he retorted "What green?"

Do-it-yourself is even less up his street. He does basic jobs around the house, from changing light bulbs to washing-up, and compared with those who can't boil an egg he is quite a practical man; but he could never put up shelves or build walls, or anything similar, having been a dunce in woodwork and metalwork at school, always far behind the others.

Regarding shopping, he pities the bowlers whose wives drag them round fashionable emporiums in spare time at championships and tournaments, usually without buying a thing. He would never let Olga inflict that on him, although at home he is not averse to going to Sainsbury's. At least, he says, that's useful, unlike window-shopping, which is a waste of shoe leather and an unnecessary trial of patience.

That leaves travel. When club members return from holiday and announce "I've been to Disneyland" or "I've been on a Caribbean cruise," and then ask Uncle Fred where he went, he takes pleasure, even pride, in replying "Oh, Hastings, as a matter of fact." And it's true. He's not one for foreign travel, having a fellow-feeling for the man he read about (he's forgotten who it was) who said that he wouldn't mind seeing China if he could come back the same day. Uncle Fred is happy where he is, doing what he's doing, which, nine times out of ten – well, seven times, to be realistic – concerns bowls in some way.

At the moment he's busy organising short-mat bowling at his club during the winter. This is good fun and, more important in Uncle Fred's view, improves touch and control. Uncle Fred likes short jacks in the real game in any case, and believes them to be the best method of "throwing" the opposition when his side is in trouble. He says any bowler of average ability can play to a long jack, but that it is the mark of an above average bowler to adapt successfully to a short one.

He once saw his old friend Les win the club's singles final by changing to minimum jacks when he was 5–19 down. Les, now dead, is remembered for his graphic absorption, while remaining on the mat, in every wood he delivered. As the bias took over, so Les's body would turn gradually in the same direction, as if biased itself, his right hand waving and the toe of his right shoe moving like the second hand of a clock.

*        *        *

All human life is there, ran the old newspaper advertisement, and Uncle Fred will tell you, with a mite of exaggeration, that it is all there in his club. He has known a few off-the-green scandals in his time, but they're predictable, and it is the little personal idiosyncrasies that amuse him much more.

Take the lady member who claims to know the horoscope of everybody in the club. Uncle Fred being a Virgo, she assures him that he did absolutely the right thing in marrying Olga, an Aries. "Even if I didn't know you," she has told him, "I could still see you're a Virgo from the way you behave on the green." "What about Reg?" Uncle Fred might ask, to draw her out. "Oh, he's a Capricorn, plain as the nose on your face." "And Bert?" "A Libra to his fingertips."

Then there is the man who buys a pipe wherever he goes to play in a tournament. This has nothing to do with Bryant's example; it's just an odd habit he's got into. He does, all the same, have a special affection for the pipe he bought in Clevedon. His wife died a few years ago and he spends part of each summer now at various tournaments, adding to his collection of pipes and also to his topographical knowledge, for he loves exploring seaside towns on foot; he's not one of those narrow people who only want to play. After a day's bowling at Worthing he will enjoy a meal and a pint alone in the Egremont and then set off along the front, returning to his hotel at nightfall. That is what he calls a perfect day for a man in his circumstances.

One of the social members, who lived a long time in America, wears a cowboy-style hat and does not always remember to remove it in the clubhouse. His favourite seat is at the corner of the bar farthest from the entrance, and as he leans there, a quiet man with a drooping moustache, you could imagine him in a Dodge City saloon. They call him Tex, and when he speaks the accent chimes.

Uncle Fred possesses a copy of the centenary booklet of the North London club and relishes quoting from it this passage about a past president, Harry Summers: "Harry was a Northumbrian and had been a farmer and farm consultant; he was a man who told many a tale and his claim to have been the first man to take a bull into a china shop was subject to doubt amongst the members until he produced a photograph, taken in a well-known china shop in Bond Street, to prove it."

"Mr. Summers would have been a credit to our club," Uncle Fred says.

*     *     *

Uncle Fred possesses something unusual among club bowlers: a certain sense of the game's history. He collects EBA *Yearbooks* and of a winter evening, as if to banish the cold outside the window and bring the glow of summer into the room, likes to browse among the championship records, remembering this or that final, and seeing, in the names of the great players down the years, the beginning and end of eras, from Carruthers, through Wade and Baker and Allen, to Bryant and Line and Allcock. He never, or rarely, talks of all this to anyone; but it is a part of him, and by no means the least part.

Naturally there are limits to this historical interest of his. He is not curious about the various theories concerning where, how or when the game began, or what kings and queens of England played it. It exists, and that is enough for him. His eyes light up only when he comes to Mitchell and his pioneering laws in the middle of the last century – the birth of the game as everybody now knows it. In short, Uncle Fred's interest is really a player's interest, practical, though with a dash of modern romance, a vision of the thousands of journeys begun in all corners of the land in May and unwinding, round by round, to the summit, the national championships, in August.

So when his own club required an outside honours board, Uncle Fred was just the man to arrange it. For years there was no justification for such a board, nobody having won appropriate honours, partly, according to Uncle Fred, because they lacked competitive fibre. But fortunes changed, a few wins at area and county level started to come the club's way, some inspired by Uncle Fred, and he it was who made sure the board was duly erected, giving visitors something more impressive to read during post-match meals.

"If I hadn't had that board put up," Uncle Fred said a long time afterwards, "we still wouldn't have one. We were too parochial then. Presidents and chairmen and club champions are important and deserve their gold leaf, but it's outside success that puts a club on the map and gets it known and respected. I mean, look at Clevedon. We can't be like them, but there's no harm in trying."

His club now has a passable record in outside competitions; nothing national yet, but who knows? Uncle Fred may not live to see that day, but meanwhile he can dip into his yearbooks again and indulge a dream or two.

\*     \*     \*

A game for all ages, bowls. Uncle Fred recalls seeing a news-paper photograph, taken at Radlett in Hertfordshire, of a 12-year-old boy and a 97-year-old man, both bowlers, the latter still active. Percy first picked up a bowl when he was fourteen, and there was once a member of Uncle Fred's club who lived to be 100, although he had stopped playing long before he was 97. He spent his last years in a rest home and Uncle Fred went to see him soon after his hundredth birthday and brought up the subject of bowls. The old fellow would not talk of it, preferring the Great War, in which he won the Military Medal.

He had been a good bowler in his day, good enough, some thought, to deserve an England trial, but the call never came. Nor did it come for Uncle Fred, who admits this was not an oversight on the part of the selectors. He says he would not have been up to it and that was that. He believes he would have had the "bottle" but not the skill.

Any competent player can bowl the occasional bowl that has his family and friends comparing him with Tony Allcock or Andy Thomson. Allcock and Thomson, however, produce such bowls often and almost as a matter of course. What's more, they produce them in the heat of national and international competition, not just in club championships.

The other day Uncle Fred was watching a husband and wife practising on a local green. The wife is an international, her husband is not, and both have the same style of delivery – a point noted by the man sitting beside Uncle Fred. "Yes," Uncle Fred said, "but not the same hands. If he had her hands he'd be as consistent as her. It's a tactile game – it's all in the 'feel' and 'feel' can't be coached into a bowler. You either have it or you don't. You can have a perfect delivery but if you don't have the 'feel' you won't get very far. The best players have the 'feel' of the best pianists."

The husband is a civil servant, rather precise in all things, including bowls, which bears out Uncle Fred's theory of a correlation between a man's job and his approach to the game. He has been known to guess, with a fair degree of accuracy, what a man does for a living from his appearance and behaviour on the green; and if he turns out to be wrong, it is not usually by much – for example, mistaking an accountant for a banker.

But he has noticed that guessing is getting harder, and blames computers, which have taken over so many jobs that, according to him, the people who use them are coming to look more and more alike in dress and expression. Percy tinkers a lot with computers, considers them a boon, and rejects his father's notion as hopelessly far-fetched. "Do I look like everybody else?" he asks. "Not yet," Uncle Fred murmurs.

*          *          *

Uncle Fred has made countless speeches in his time, without ever being bothered by shyness or claiming to be in the Lincoln or Churchill mould. If speaking ability were the sole criterion, he'd make an ideal EBA president. Most of his speeches have been after club matches or at annual meetings, the latter much more difficult than the former.

Post-match speeches couldn't be easier, according to Uncle Fred. If they were paid for he'd be ashamed to take the money, since the sentiments are always the same, and in his opinion it would be wiser to record them, like British Rail announcements, and save the breath of a thousand speakers. Yet Uncle Fred prefers to do the speaking, for one simple reason: if he had to listen he'd be bored rigid. From which you will gather that there are limits to his liking for tradition.

At least there is variety to speeches at annual meetings. All is not always for the best in the best of possible worlds on those occasions. "The lads" are not always "a great bunch". The club might be in the red, a couple of members might come to blows, the president might resign because of trouble at home, meaning divorce. As for keeping order, that presents no problem for a man of Uncle Fred's standing. Nobody has done more for the club than he has; he is liked, respected, and, in a few cases, feared; and his voice carries above the loudest uproar. He was not a sergeant-major for nothing.

A few times, also, Uncle Fred has been asked to deliver the address at the funerals of club members. Now that is difficult. But Uncle Fred responds to a challenge, even one so delicate, and some of the bereaved relatives have gone out of their way afterwards to express their genuine appreciation of what he said. Partly this may be because he would never speak at the funeral of someone he had not known well; never take knowledge of the person at second hand. And the relatives sense it.

Uncle Fred once saw, at Gravesend, a gravestone with the inscription: "To the memory of Mr Alderman Nynn. An honest man and an excellent bowler." He noted it down and is toying with the idea of inserting a clause in his will that his own memorial should contain those words.

\*       \*       \*

Uncle Fred enjoys his food and has a good but not excessive, appetite. Bowls doesn't take it out of you physically to any marked extent, but even so, if you go on the green without stoking up beforehand, you're unlikely to play well. Uncle Fred hasn't forgotten losing a pairs final because his lead hadn't eaten since breakfast and bowled short end after end, leaving Uncle Fred to try to retrieve, which even he couldn't do every time.

Olga is a semi-vegetarian, which means that she will eat fish and eggs in small amounts but no meat. Uncle Fred is a self-styled theoretical vegetarian; he would like to give up meat, for vaguely humanitarian reasons, but can't break a lifetime's habit, and in any case he dislikes leaf vegetables ("rabbit food") and eats only potatoes, parsnips, tomatoes, mushrooms and, at a stretch, peas.

Match meals consisting far too often of salad, Uncle Fred is rarely able to clear his plate, unless he can pass on the

lettuce to his neighbour. It is better for him during the indoor
season, when salads are inappropriate, and the main course
is usually roast beef and Yorkshire pudding or sausage and
mash – something robust.

Breakfast is Uncle Fred's favourite – he calls it the king
of meals. Yet it is only when he is away from home, perhaps staying in a hotel during a seaside tournament, that he
indulges in a full English breakfast – what's referred to by
some as "the works" or "a full house". At home he restricts
himself to orange juice and cereal, with the occasional egg.
Ham or cheese rolls he finds sufficient in the middle of
the day, and he has his main meal at night, provided, of
course, that he doesn't have a match then. If so, he tem-
porarily reorganises his eating habits, being a firm believer
in putting bowls first and fitting lesser matters such as food
round it.

Uncle Fred doesn't suggest for a moment that the diet
outlined above is the best for bowlers, let alone that it is a
winning one. Players overeat or undereat and still win championships. There is room for all sorts; Uncle Fred's doctor has
another bowler-patient who enjoys excellent health though his
bowels move only twice a week. Uncle Fred was incredulous
when he heard that: but it is true.

And what of Percy? He'll eat anything and everything
without putting on weight, while others have only to look
at a cream cake to go up a stone. He likes pub meals most of
all, the portions large, the surroundings sociable and smokey,
a snooker table at hand where he can pass the time that his
father keeps telling him would be better spent on the bowling
green.

\*       \*       \*

Uncle Fred bowled with lignums when he started in the game
and was quite successful with them, but he uses something
more modern now – Henselite, Vitalite, Tyrolite or, as he
adds with a wink, Corstrikealite. Yet not so modern as to

be straight-running. His woods take a full traditional swing which it gratifies him to watch. Without that swing it is not the true game, according to him. "Reduce the bias and you reduce the skill," he asserts; "and if you reduce the skill that much, you might as well stop bowling altogether and concentrate on gin rummy."

Talking of swing reminds him of a friend of his, Nico, who lives at Seascale in Cumbria. Nico writes books about a game with another kind of swing, cricket, and has never, to Uncle Fred's knowledge, played bowls. They exchange letters periodically and Nico had this to say in his most recent:

"It was during my cricket-watching last summer that I kept coming across underarm bowlers. First at Painswick ('It's the oldest green in the country') during the Cheltenham festival and then at Abergavenny ('We're the oldest club in Wales – older than Cardiff') during the annual county championship match there. The Gloucestershire flag flew from the adjacent bowls green and they made me very much at home."

Uncle Fred's club once had cricket and tennis sections, but they went long ago, which is unusual, the bowls as a rule being the one to go under in such cases. There is a club in Uncle Fred's area where that indeed happened a year or two back, the bowls perishing while the cricket and tennis continued to thrive, and Uncle Fred, when he passes it now, feels depressed at the sight of the once-busy green overgrown and desolate.

At his own club the bowls and tennis sections had shared the same pavilion, the cricket being down the field. There was of course a bit of friction, the lissom tennis set rather condescending to the creakier bowlers, and the bowlers returning service, so to speak, with a sort of vague resentment. Partly our old friend the generation gap. So when the tennis and cricket folded owing to dwindling membership, the bowlers were chuffed.

There are few left to remember those days – by general consent those bad old days – of joint tenancy. They were a little before Uncle Fred's time, but that doesn't prevent him drawing conclusions and pointing morals, saying that under no circumstances should dissimilar sports share the same premises, and that if anything like it recurred at his club he would do the unthinkable and pack up bowling. Mock expressions of shock-horror invariably greet this announcement, everyone knowing that Uncle Fred could no more pack up bowling than the sun could rise in the west.

*　　　　　*　　　　　*

Just to prove there are nooks and crannies in Uncle Fred's life not filled by the game of bowls, let me tell you that he enjoys the occasional day at the races. Being cautious, though not mean, he never bets. It's the social and sartorial side of things that he goes for, and the food, and the space, and the spectacle. He went to the Derby years ago but could not get close enough to see much more than the horses' ears and the jockeys' heads flashing by, and he now prefers small meetings such as Plumpton.

He has never sat on a horse but once found himself standing beside Red Rum and would have sat on him for the experience if it had been allowed. Red Rum had been brought to the opening of a betting shop in Uncle Fred's high street on a Saturday morning. A crowd gathered and in due course one of Ginger McCain's vans appeared round the corner and stopped in a side road.

Red Rum stood on the pavement for about ten minutes, an object of admiration and curiosity, and was then taken inside for the official opening ceremony. As soon as that was over, the crowd were let in to make more fuss of the quadruped and to put questions to his connections. How old is he? Does he have a good appetite? How does he pass the time? Is he still healthy? How often does he appear in public now? Red Rum did not stir a hoof while all this was going on. He is used to the interiors of betting shops and to the caressing hands of punters on his nose. Uncle Fred recalls thinking that he had expected to see a bigger horse, one more obviously capable of getting round Aintree year after year.

Later he told Olga about Red Rum and she regretted having missed him. "More interesting than a lot of your silly old bowlers," she said. "I thought you might say that" was his rejoinder.

Uncle Fred also enjoys a day in the parks, perhaps catching the train to Victoria and the bus to Baker Street before walking through Regents Park, pausing beside the boules pitch on the way, and over Primrose Hill to Hampstead, where he and Olga know a slightly raffish little place that does items like scrambled eggs with smoked salmon and waffles with syrup. Then, if they feel specially energetic, they might cross the Heath to Kenwood, turning for home at the top of Highgate High Street.

It would not be true to say that during these hours Uncle Fred never gives a thought to bowls; but he has sufficient tact not to mention it. Such outings help to keep him fit, and that means, as the first priority, being fit for the next match. That's how he looks at it.

*       *       *

Although bowls is becoming, every year, a game for younger people, health continues to be a recurrent topic of conversation in dressing-rooms: but not with Uncle Fred. He attributes his freedom from hernias, arthritis, and other scourges of age to the fact that he chose robust parents and was lucky in his genes. He is also gentle with himself, observing moderation in food, drink, and tobacco.

But most of all he attributes his health to bowls. To him it is an elixir and he cannot understand why doctors don't acknowledge as much by recommending it to patients, as they would any other cure or preventative. He once made this point to his own doctor, who seemed to think it a sound idea, but whether he acted on it Uncle Fred doesn't know: the two men haven't met, professionally or socially, for quite a while.

Bowls, according to Uncle Fred, is far more beneficial than pills and tonics. He instances the case of Ted, a neighbour, who joined his club on being made redundant. Ted's work, entailing frequent travel, had given him little time to do anything else. He was overweight, a prey to minor illnesses, and usually among the first to go down in any epidemic. After a couple of seasons on the green he was a changed man. He lost a stone and a half during a particularly hot summer, bowling on while others sat gasping in the shade, and his general health is now good.

R. T. Harrison wrote that bowling is the best exercise in the world for the kidneys. R. C. Robertson-Glasgow, asking what pastime is best "when you have become just a stuffed shirt on the cricket field," described bowls as "an admirable, sociable and dignified game, but severe on the kidneys." The author of an anonymous letter to a bowling magazine said it is "good for all disorders of the liver; and for pains in the loins, loss of appetite, shortness of breath, nervous exhaustion, gout and toothache it is unsurpassed."

Uncle Fred is proud to say that illness has never compelled him to miss a match. Now and again he might not have felt one hundred per cent, but he always turned up. The only operation he has ever had was to remove his tonsils and adenoids, and that was in his school days. He has a feeling, amounting almost to a superstition, that, in the unlikely event of his requiring another operation, it will mean the end of his bowling career. "That," he declares "would be the twenty-second end for me."

# Afterword

Woods "enchanted" – why so?

The dictionary says that enchanted means bewitched and that bewitched means affected by magic. There have been, I trust, more than a few enchanted or bewitched woods in this book, woods bowled by every sort of player, from world champion to absolute beginner. For we have all, at one time or another, bowled enchanted woods, those that gave us the sudden thrill of certainty that they were going to be perfect shots, and made us feel, for a blissful moment, like David Bryant at his zenith.

Ever the realist, Uncle Fred, my old friend and informal conduit, through whom I have been able to say things about the game that I might not otherwise have had the chance of saying, put the matter in perspective: "Any competent player can bowl the occasional bowl that has his family and friends comparing him with Tony Allcock or Andy Thomson. But Allcock and Thomson produce such bowls often and almost as a matter of course. What's more, they produce them in the heat of national and international competition, not just in club championships."

And as you know by now, Uncle Fred, club bowler extraordinaire, remembers, or claims to remember, his own very first wood, on his first day on the green, half a century ago at least, and how it ended up a dead-length toucher. He called it a revelation. He might with equal truth have called it enchanted.

Finis.